FENG SHUI

Discover
Money, Health
and
Love

FENG SHUI

Discover
Money, Health
and Love

Master Larry Sang's System

written by

Mark Douglas Marfori

▲ Dragon Publishing

Santa Monica, California USA

FENG SHUI

Discover Money, Health and Love

Master Larry Sang's System

written by

Mark Douglas Marfori

Published by: **Dragon Publishing**
1223 Broadway, #231
Santa Monica, Ca. 90404   U.S.A.
310/285-8616

Copyright © 1993 Mark Douglas Marfori

ISBN :   0-9637748-4-0
$13.95 Softcover

This is the incense burner at Tsi Lai Temple, Hacienda Heights Ca. The temple was designed incorporating Feng Shui principles.

If you live on a hilly street, make sure you are protected against excessive water runoff. It is considered especially bad Feng Shui if the water is dirty. Dirty water runoff brings poor finances.

Table of Contents

How to Get the Most From this Book

1. Read Carefully. You may want to scan the book quickly the first time you read it. Still, to learn thoroughly and understand the information contained in this book requires several readings. Stop and think about the material presented. Feng Shui is an art slowly mastered over time.

2. Commit Yourself to Learning the Art of Feng Shui. The saying "a little knowledge can be dangerous" is most appropriate in the practice of Feng Shui. The knowledge contained herein should not be taken lightly. Remember that true masters of Feng Shui have spent entire lifetimes mastering the art.

3. Let the power of Feng Shui prove itself. Keep an open mind as you progress through this book. When you become competent enough to integrate some principles into your life, judge it's worth by the result. Don't mix the ideas presented here with other schools of Feng Shui.

4. Finally, be of service to others. Make a pledge to improve not only your life with Feng Shui, but all those who cross your path in need of help. Give the knowledge of Feng Shui to others whenever you can and see your life enriched a hundredfold!

Please Read this Information

This book provides information regarding the subject matter covered. The authors are not engaged in rendering legal, medical or other professional advice. If you need medical or legal advice, a competent professional should be called. Feng Shui is not a get-rich quick or cure-all scheme. Changes in your life will happen as fast as you are ready for them. Be patient in your study of Feng Shui.

The authors have tried to make this book as complete and accurate as possible. However, there may be typographical and content mistakes. Use this book as a general guide. Do not use it as the final authority and ultimate source of Feng Shui knowledge.

This book was written to educate and entertain. The authors, publisher, distributors and the American Feng Shui Society shall have neither liability nor responsibility to any person with respect to any loss or damage caused, or alleged to be caused by this book.

Master Larry Sang is considered one of the foremost authorities on Feng Shui. His clients include some of the business world's biggest industrialists, international film celebrities and government leaders. Retired from active practice, Master Sang is devoting his efforts to spreading the knowledge of Feng Shui through his books and lectures.

Raised in Hong Kong, he has been practicing over 25 years. He consulted with the most prominent residents of Hong Kong before coming to the United States. Master Sang founded the non-profit American Feng Shui Institute and the American Society of Feng Shui to further the knowledge and practice of Feng Shui. He has also conducted classes at the University of Southern California and Northrop University in Los Angeles.

Master Sang periodically hosts a Feng Shui and Astrology radio program and is a regular contributor to Chinese astrological magazines. Also renowned for his calligraphy and painting, Master Sang resides in Monterey Park, California with his wife and children.

Mark D. Marfori discovered the mysterious art of Feng Shui on one of his business trips to Asia. Himself a Filipino-American, he became intrigued by the practices of his Asian colleagues and was prompted to begin studying Feng Shui in 1983. This book is the culmination of his study, using the knowledge and practices of Master Larry Sang.

Mark, a former professional with Toyota and Anheuser-Busch Corporations is a graduate of UCLA and MBA holder from the University of Southern California. He now spends much of his time studying Chinese philosophy and is hard at work on an advanced sequel to this book. Projects in the works also include a book on the fascinating practices of Chinese face reading and palmistry.

Mr. Marfori continues to consult with clients involved in international finance, real estate development and government. Mark also publishes a monthly newsletter on Feng Shui and assists Master Sang through the American Society of Feng Shui. He resides in Santa Monica, California with his wife Riza.

ACKNOWLEDGEMENTS

Many people help on a venture of this size. My sincerest thanks go to all who helped in any way, big or small. In particular, David Twicken deserves special mention for his help above and beyond the call of duty. His expert advice, particularly on the subject of Taoism was most appreciated. Mary MacMannes was my style editor and was always standing by to offer her assistance. We owe you one Mary!

It would take several pages to name everyone who helped on this project. However, several who deserve mention include Chris Nolt of Cirrus Design for her technical assistance, and Robert Howard who produced the cover design. My good friend Gary (the answer man) Clark stayed on call to support me whenever my computer refused to cooperate.

Thanks go to my Chinese medicine man, Dr. Douglas Kihn who helped keep me healthy in body and mind. Gratitude to my mom and dad for always believing in me. Finally, my wife Riza encouraged and prodded me past the tough parts. Without her this book wouldn't have been possible.

Mark Douglas Marfori

FOREWORD

Feng Shui, figuratively meaning "natural science" in Chinese is the traditional art of creating a harmonious environment. Feng Shui will show you how to create a safe and healthy home and enliven your living space. Most importantly, Feng Shui will transform your home, workplace or business into a center of personal power.

Using Feng Shui can improve your health, relationships and overall prosperity by finding your best living space within the natural order of the universe. Feng Shui is based on ideas presented in the I-Ching using mathematical and astronomical calculations.

Feng Shui is based on the idea that all living things in the universe are governed by the environment. The most important part of our environment is the universal energy known as "Chi". Feng Shui can help you direct this universal energy in a way that promotes harmony, prosperity and good health. The natural elements of our environment, which interact with "Chi" currents and Earth's magnetic fields form the basis of this book.

Congratulations on the wise decision you have made to help yourself and others with the proven ideas presented in this book. Warmest wishes for abundance in all areas of your life.

Master Larry Sang

Tsi Lai Temple was designed so that it faces out
to a valley and sits against a mountain.

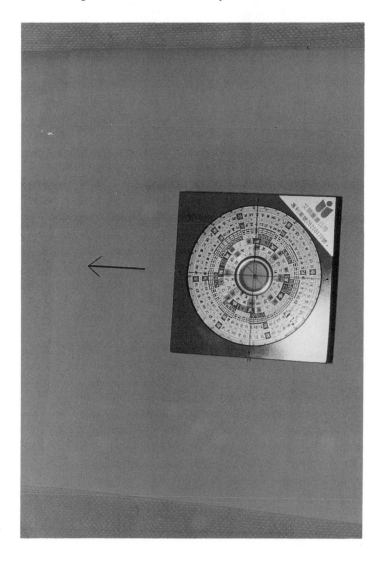

Traditional Chinese Geomancer's Compass.
A compass reading is the mandatory first step in a traditional Feng Shui reading. This compass is now available in English.

Chapter One

A FASCINATING LOOK AT THE ORIGINS OF FENG SHUI

Chinese calligraphy meaning Feng Shui

For over 2,000 years, the ancient art of Feng Shui has been an important part of Chinese culture. This book hopes to spread the ancient wisdom of Feng Shui to all people seeking a happier and healthier life. The benefits of Feng Shui, once restricted only to the rich and powerful of China, are yours for the asking. If you seek more harmony, peace and balance in your life, Feng Shui can help show the way. With all the challenges facing our contemporary world, Feng Shui seems even more relevant today. The world's rush into the 21 century seems more at odds with environmental and health concerns. Perhaps practical wisdom from the past can help us find the answers to our present and future problems.

Feng Shui is an element of traditional Chinese philosophy that harmoniously relates a person to his environment. Chinese philosophers divide the potential of a human life into a matrix of possibilities. Feng Shui is one aspect affecting the possibilities of a person's life.

The most important factor has traditionally been the destiny of a person defined by his astrological horoscope. The horoscope outlines the general "direction" and genealogy of your life. It defines your tendencies, weaknesses and strengths. A person is not completely controlled by the horoscope. Tendencies can be overcome and weaknesses minimized through effort. Still, there are limitations placed on you by your horoscope. For example, you may attain a comfortable lifestyle through hard work, but you won't become a millionaire if your birth chart does not show great material wealth. Improving yourself to the best of your ability is your responsibility.

Second in importance is a person's "luck." The "breaks" in life can be largely attributed to persistence and a positive state of mind. Luck can result from maximizing the other four life factors. For example, hard work, good deeds, and Feng Shui can improve your luck.

Third in importance is the art of Feng Shui. To use an analogy, a plowhorse may never become a champion racehorse, but hard work, persistence and Feng Shui, may produce a very fast plowhorse. Think of Feng Shui as improving the relationship with our living environment. Using Feng Shui harmonizes our living space. This positive relationship can improve your health, wealth potential and family relations.

Fourth in importance are the "good works" done throughout a lifetime. Every great book on philosophy and religion, says that selfless giving and charity creates it's own rewards. Performing charitable acts is best when you don't expect anything in return. If you find your life lacking in any way, try giving that which you want, without any thought of a payoff.

Finally, there is the importance of effort, commonly known as hard work. The most prosperously aspected destiny won't become a reality without a serious effort. Good luck merely places opportunities in our path. It's up to you to seize the opportunity and run with it.

YOUR LIFE'S COURSE
(order   of   importance)

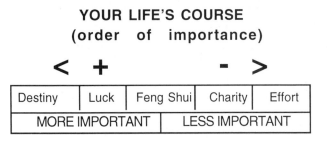

Destiny	Luck	Feng Shui	Charity	Effort
MORE IMPORTANT			LESS IMPORTANT	

By maximizing your luck, performing good works, giving a strong effort and using Feng Shui, you can overcome many of the negatives of your destiny. We all have the power and freedom to shape a large part of our destiny.

Feng Shui has only been known in the West for a short time. Unfortunately, because of the secretive tradition of Feng Shui, some superstitious practices surround it. One goal of this book is to present to you, the true essence of traditional Feng Shui. As you progress through this book, keep in mind that the true science of Feng Shui remains timeless, positive and powerful. Let the knowledge in this book help you in your life's journey.

BACKGROUND

The Chinese, part of the oldest, continuous culture in the world, have always struggled to live in harmony with nature. The China of today, as yesterday, remains largely an agrarian nation with most people living close to the land. Survival for many always meant an accommodation with Mother Nature.

Through keen observation and practical wisdom, accumulated over the last 3,000 years, a practical body of knowledge for healthy living has evolved. This ancient wisdom, originally called *K'an Yu*, has enabled it's users to live more harmoniously within their living environment. Although many people of today's world cluster in large cities and choose to work indoors, the science of Feng Shui remains just as useful as ever.

Feng Shui, literally meaning "Wind and Water," is a method to unite the earthly dimensions of time, environment, people and man-made structures into a healthy balance. The following illustration shows how Feng Shui unites these factors into a blueprint for harmonious living.

Factors Used in Feng Shui Analysis

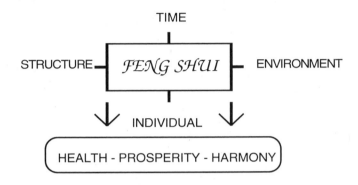

The **environment** factor considers the internal and external components of a structure. For example, how is the general energy (Chi) flow? Do other man-made or natural factors affect the building?   The **time** factor analyzes the changes in magnetic energy within your home or office. Major energy shifts occurring in daily, monthly, annual and twenty year cycles affect your health, relationships, and finances. Every **structure** has a specific energy depending on the construction date. Factors such as the facing direction, floorplan, interior design and furnishings must be considered. Finally, a **person's** individual energy based on his/her birthday is analyzed.   Every person has an energy form which interacts positively or negatively with other energy sources.

As you can see, the practice of Feng Shui can be a complex and serious study when done professionally. This book will examine these factors and analyze them in a context useful to your daily life.

Within nature, there exists an optimum location and time for a person to live your life. Feng Shui exists as a framework and guide for harmonious living. Although the I-Ching is the major source of Feng Shui, a large portion has developed from "good, common sense."

The true art of Feng Shui is *not* a religion *nor* does it advocate any mystical practices. The basis of Feng Shui is scientific, with over 3,000 years of empirical evidence. It doesn't conflict with any religion and is based upon natural science. Feng Shui serves only to uplift and benefit the whole of humanity.

Science has long acknowledged that magnetic fields cover earth. You probably remember your elementary science primer that explained the nature of earth's magnetism. Magnetism, essentially, is a force of attraction. It also can act as a repelling force. You can easily prove its existence yourself with an inexpensive compass.

The ancients observed that earth's magnetic fields affected man in a positive or negative manner, depending on the date and their position relative to the magnetic fields. Essentially, the masters were saying that the flow of energy (Chi) is not a random phenomenon. Like everything within nature, there is a cycle of energy ordered by time and existing in specific channels. To go against the energy flow creates disharmony and portends disease, and misfortune. Positioning yourself in a positive way with the magnetic energy that surrounds us has the opposite effect.

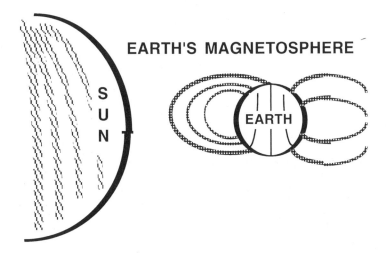

EARTH'S MAGNETOSPHERE

SUN

EARTH

Traditionally, Feng Shui advocates that the energy force existing within and without all of us can act in harmony or disharmony to a person.   The earth's magnetic polar forces act as a channel for this energy source.

Chi is a "current" that permeates our universe. Chi exists as the primal energy source within all living things. The flow of Chi is governed by many environmental factors, although it exits in unity with our bodily Chi. Chi energy is the same whether it flows in or out of the human body.

It's widely believed in the east and more recently in the west that Chi can be guided and manipulated within the body.   Acupuncture, an accepted modality of the American Medical Association can testify to this. Feng Shui when properly applied, manipulates Chi in a way that positively affects a person.

The ancients observed over thousands of years that correct alignment within the earth's magnetic fields and correct manipulation of Chi foster harmony, prosperity and long life. As you progress through this book and integrate some ideas into your life, judge the power of this knowledge by your results.

Negative energy can project onto a
house at the end of a dead-end street.

HISTORY

The origins of Feng Shui can be traced back several thousand years. From 475-770 B.C., the practices of Feng Shui were compiled into a common body of thought. The accepted principles, still, are known to predate this period by at least 1,000 years. Books on the subject were published as early as 25 A.D., during the Han dynasty. Imperial scholars theorized and wrote on various subjects of Feng Shui as early as the Song Dynasty (960 B.C.).

FENG SHUI HISTORICAL TIMELINE

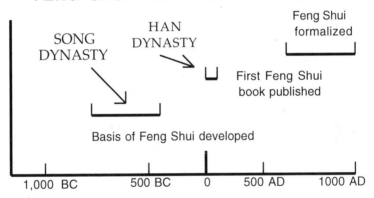

Classical Feng Shui is divided into the Yin House and the Yang House. The Yin House is Feng Shui for the deceased. The Yang House is a guide for the living. The importance and reverence for the dead in Chinese culture is well known. Yet, little is known or said about the importance of Feng Shui to the dead. Those seeking knowledge about the Yin House aspects of Feng Shui may want to read other advanced Feng Shui books by the same author. Many in China believe that the siting of the grave site directly affects the living descendants. The positioning and timing of the living (Yang House) is the more popularly known aspect of Feng Shui.

Traditionally, Feng Shui has remained in the hands of the rich and powerful. In imperial China, all Feng Shui Masters were in the employ of the emperor. Masters were not permitted to be outside the control of the royal court. The emperors feared that public knowledge of Feng Shui would strengthen enemies of the realm. All Feng Shui subject matter was secured within the palace for use only by the court appointed masters.

The masters of the art were handsomely compensated by the court and other powerful people. Consequently, not many masters eagerly shared their knowledge. Historically, Feng Shui Masters have kept knowledge of Feng Shui within the family. The turbulent history of China has reinforced this tradition.

Apprentices, usually limited to only one son were few and trained for much of their lives before they could be designated as a master. This tradition of secrecy continues to this day.

It's generally recognized within the world of Feng Shui that few genuine masters of the art exist today. Most reside outside the People's Republic of China primarily in Taiwan and Hong Kong.

EARLY FENG SHUI MASTERS

The compilation and formalization of Feng Shui can be attributed to four family groups, each with its own unique interpretation. The four families are: Young, Sang, Liu and Lai. These four families continue to this day through their present descendants as acknowledged masters of the art and science of Feng Shui. The practices presented in this book are from the same school as the original four families.

This book brings to you the classical method of Feng Shui. Some parts such as Yin/Yang are borrowed from the I-Ching. Much of the rest of this school of Feng Shui developed from ancient beliefs and practices indigenous to China.

This is the first public presentation of these methods. There are several other popular schools of Feng Shui with many adherents that exist today. Most practitioners and adherents are in Asian countries with large communities of expatriate Chinese.

Since the inception of Feng Shui, the imperial court of China has sought to limit the knowledge of Feng Shui. Knowledge of the subject did manage to escape imperial control. In the Five Dynasties period (907 B.C.), during the Yellow Bandit Rebellion, Master Young, the Imperial Court Meteorologist escaped to a remote province during a period of extreme unrest. This was the first time Feng Shui knowledge was removed from the Forbidden City.

With his books and personal knowledge, Master Young sought, throughout his lifetime, to serve and help the people of China. Master Young apprenticed Master Sang, who in turn instructed Master Liu and Master Lai in the principles of Feng Shui. For centuries after the Yellow Bandit Rebellion, much of Feng Shui was known as the Young-Sang theory.

OTHER INFLUENCES

Feng Shui has incorporated several important ideas from the **I-Ching**. The **I-Ching**, also known as "The Book of Changes," is reflected throughout traditional Chinese philosophy. It's a practical guide to living. The I-Ching isn't part of any religion and acts as a framework pointing to an effective way of life. Think of it as a "road map" for realizing and living a healthy life.

The balance necessary for an effective life is often described through the idea of Yin-Yang. The idea of Yin-Yang is an integral part of Chinese philosophy. It states that harmony exits when there is balance. This could apply to your health, career and family. When we live in an unbalanced way, negativity is more prone in our lives. This imbalance is manifested in such forms as overwork, drug addiction and lack of exercise.

Yin-Yang Balance

Yang	Yin
Active, Masculine	Recessive, Feminine

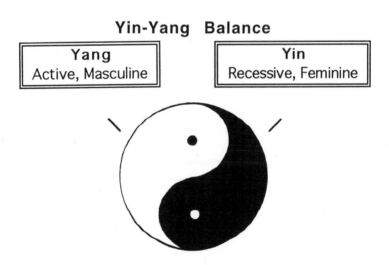

An imbalance commonly occurs because of emotional problems or unhealthy cultural and negative attitudes. For example, anger and hostility can often weaken the body's defenses and cause various diseases. Restoring the Yin/Yang balance can strengthen the body and help it ward off disease.

Feng Shui seeks balance in the same way. Through siting and use of Chi modifiers, you can harmonize your environment. Excessive or stagnant Chi results in disease and disharmony. A balance of Yin-Yang is desired for optimum longevity, prosperity and health.

The idea of five elements consisting of fire, water, metal, wood and earth is also borrowed from the I-Ching. This deceptively simple classification system enables a master to categorize the types of Chi energy.

All things on earth belong to one of the five groups and express an energy unique to their element. For example, a home that has a weak metal energy can affect the occupants through lung, chest and head disorders.

Traditional 5 Elements

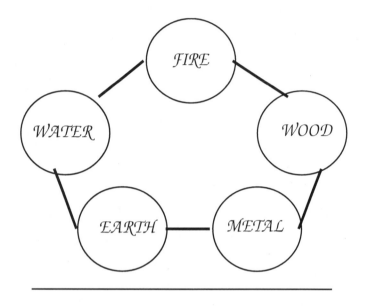

CHI ENERGY

Chi is an ancient idea conceived originally by the ancient Chinese philosophers. Chi is an energy force that permeates our bodies and the air we breathe. Chi also exists as matter, which is it's densest form. Chinese physicians explain that the body ages because Chi energy depletes throughout a lifetime.

Within the realm of Feng Shui, Chi can affect the human body in a positive or negative manner. For example, the illustration below show rooms with and without an overhead beam.

Chi is also an airborne energy, and in the room with a drop ceiling, the energy moves in unbroken and even currents. Looking at the room with a beam, you can see that the Chi flow is disrupted and dispersed in an uneven manner. Because of the Chi disruption, a person who lives, sleeps or works in such a room will be affected negatively because of disruptions in the natural Chi flow.

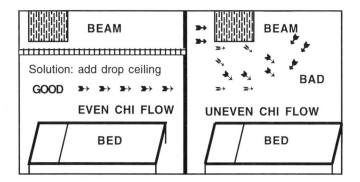

Traditional Chinese physicians believe that disruptions, blockages, excessive or insufficient Chi flow will result in diseases of the mind, body or emotions. Your Chi can be strengthened with Feng Shui. With a positive mindset your Chi can be developed and changed into a higher spiritual force.

Specific medical anomalies associated with misdirected Chi also can be a function of direction. For example, negative Chi associated with southerly magnetic currents will result in ophthalmic disorders or heart disease. Specific diseases are associated with the direction of the Chi current. This subject will be covered in greater detail in the following chapters. Chinese physicians have taught that disease is but a symptom of disharmonious Chi. Once you know your Chi you can nurture, sustain and protect it.

When you are in good health, your metabolism and internal secretions are functioning properly. Your Chi is correctly aligned and you feel energetic and happy. This state regenerates itself and sustains health. Although we in the West like to think of the physical, mental and spiritual aspects as separate human components, they are all interconnected. These factors affect each other as outlined in oriental medicine.

Chinese physicians believe that if you strengthen your physical energy, you can grow spiritually. The general effect is to attain a balance of physical, spiritual and mental Chi. A balanced life portends happiness, health, prosperity and long life.

SUMMARY

The essence of Feng Shui is the proper circulation of Chi through techniques that harmonize the flow of positive Chi.   Chinese physicians, from whom the principle of Chi is borrowed, know that a healthy body produces and possesses healthy Chi.   An unhealthy body possesses and produces unhealthy Chi.

Negative Chi in your living and work environment causes disease in the physical, mental and emotional parts of your being. For example, consider a beautiful plant in your house. Your body is like the planter. The planter is filled with water that represents Chi. If the water is stagnant the plant will wither and die. Fresh water sustains the plant and keeps it looking beautiful.

Negative Chi in your living environment eventually affects the inhabitants in an unhealthy manner.   A person will often feel excessively warm, irritable and tired in this environment. These are all precursors to more serious diseases and diminishment of positive Chi energy.   Naturally, you would want to remedy this situation by reducing the negative forces or even move in a severe case.

The enlightened masters of Feng Shui have always felt that Feng Shui belongs to all people. It's a positive, universal philosophy that can enrich the lives of people and ultimately lift the whole of society to a more positive plane of existence.

Large statues and other types of ceramic pieces
can be used as an effective earth remedy.

Chapter Two

YOUR ENVIRONMENT AFFECTS YOU

Chinese calligraphy meaning *Fire*

Feng Shui is based on natural forces affecting man's harmonization and alignment with the Chi energy force. Earth's magnetic forces, easily measured by scientific instruments as simple as a compass, comprise an important element of Feng Shui theory.   Proper alignment with the earth's magnetic fields, coordinated with specific time factors will benefit you in many ways. Think of a negative alignment with earth's fields as that of two magnets. When the magnets are opposed, they force each other apart. When the poles of the magnets are aligned correctly, they will strongly attract each other.

While studying our solar system's importance in astronomy, the ancient masters observed that specific planetary movements affect the nature and movement of earth's magnetic fields. The magnetic fields in turn alter the Chi force. Although other factors play a significant role in Feng Shui, understanding Chi is the most important.

THE SOLAR SYSTEM

Astrology in Asia plays an important role in human analysis. The Chinese system resembles, but developed separately from Western astrology. Many statistical studies have shown the high correlation of major life changes with specific planetary movements. The solar system is an important aspect in understanding Feng Shui, as it is with astrology. In fact, the masters advising the imperial court were astronomers as well as Feng Shui experts. There was no delineation at that time. The basis of much of Feng Shui remains a function of specific planetary movements as a primary predictor of change.

Within the traditional school of Feng Shui (presented in this book), the planets Jupiter and Saturn are the most important.   These planets play a major role in the shaping of earth's magnetic fields. For example, Jupiter moves 30 degrees annually in its long journey around the sun. As the largest planet in the solar system, Jupiter produces changes lasting throughout the year. Of course, the annual changes themselves are different with every year. The yearly cycle operates within a larger multi-year cycle that coincides with the trigrams of the I-Ching. Jupiter and Saturn conjunctions have traditionally been the major harbingers of change affecting us here on earth. The following chart illustrates the twenty-year magnetic shift portended by the Saturn/Jupiter conjunction.

20 Year Jupiter-Saturn Conjunction

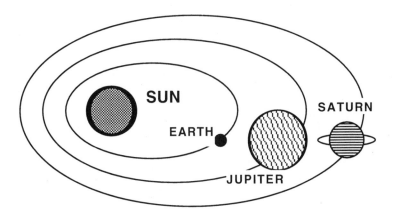

Although many types of changes can be accurately predicted based on Jupiter's yearly movement, Feng Shui also can be broken down into an eight-part cycle based on minutes, hours, days and months.

The ancients believed that Jupiter's orbit around the sun caused subtle shifts in the earth's magnetic fields. Consequently, the Chi force   realigns with every movement of Jupiter. The masters empirically observed that besides the yearly, monthly, weekly and daily changes caused by Jupiter, the biggest shift in magnetic fields occurs every twenty years. The twenty year cycle effects are enormous compared to the yearly and shorter cycles.

This major twenty year shift occurs with the conjunction of Jupiter and Saturn. A major pattern shift in earth's magnetic fields occurs every twenty years. This shift coincides with a Jupiter/Saturn alignment that causes the field shift. Again, just as in the yearly cycle, a different energy emerges every twenty years that in turn exists within a larger eight-part cycle.

EARTH'S MAGNETIC FIELDS

The primary Chi channels that cover the earth "pole to pole" are direct conduits of energy to all things that lie in their path.   Magnetism, a phenomenon closely linked with electricity, has a dual nature. It's Yin and Yang nature (positive and negative) is exhibited by Earth's polar fields. Magnetism can attract or repel substances such as iron and other elements.

The magnetic poles in the Arctic and Antarctica are known to possess enormous magnetic forces (flux). The magnetic fields display an order despite their constantly shifting motion.   In fact, scientists can chart the movement of magnetic fields that occur daily.   The Aurora Borealis, a colorful display of light visible in the polar regions, is a graphic illustration of earth's magnetism.

Each pole exerts an opposite magnetic pull. Disruptions in the magnetic field commonly affect compasses, radio and wire transmissions. Changes in the magnetic field also can be caused by common phenomena such as sunspot activity. Earth's magnetic fields serve to protect earth from excessive radiation exposure from the sun. Magnetic field flux and shifting also coincide with certain planetary movements within our solar system.

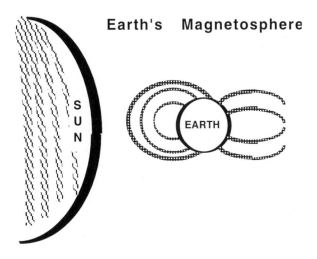

Earth's   Magnetosphere

Earth's magnetic fields are not static bodies of energy between the   twenty year Jupiter/Saturn alignments. The magnetic fields are in a constant shift. Geophysicists have been measuring the field shifts over many years. Still, their exact nature and origin are unknown to modern science. The Chinese have long observed the movement of Earth's magnetic fields. In the West we are only now evaluating the effects of various electromagnetic energies. The effect of magnetism on people is the basis of Feng Shui.

How do magnetic fields affect people? Researchers have not concluded the importance of magnetism's effect on people. The Chinese, however, have long believed that our bodies contain and react to magnetic fields.

Everything in the known universe is thought to be a form of Chi. Magnetism is but one form of Chi energy.

Only recently have scientists in the West discovered that humans possess subatomic magnetic particles within our brain tissue. Their existence has no known purpose in western science.

There is increasing evidence that exposure to electromagnetic fields may be harmful. The Chinese have maintained for many hundreds of years that exposure to negative magnetic fields encourages disease in humans. More importantly, Chinese Feng Shui prescribes a comprehensive system to detect negative magnetic fields and overcome them. Feng Shui also can provide a method to align yourself with the natural energy of Earth. By positioning yourself with Earth's natural energy forces, your overall quality of life can be improved. Feng Shui is used to improve physical health, harmonize relationships, promote peace of mind and expand material wealth.

Western scientists are today suggesting a relationship between cancer and electromagnetic fields produced by power lines and appliances. Of course, many other species of animals such as pigeons, salmon and sea mammals possess magnetic particles. The particles are believed to allow the animals to navigate earth's magnetic fields, providing an inborn sense of direction.

A Chi channel can be negative or positive depending on your placement within the channel. A negative Chi flow known as Sha can imbue a person or object with unhealthful energy. In addition, an insufficient flow of Chi acts as a negative force upon a person. Positive Chi flow is a correct alignment within the natural order of our environment. A positive living space enables a person to take in the surrounding positive energy. Think of a farmer planting his crops.   A field with plentiful water and rich soil will yield superior crops.   The farmer knows this type of field will yield an abundant crop compared to a field lacking in water and soil nutrients.

The subject of Chi manipulation will be studied in greater depth in the later chapters.   The focus of this book will be to give readers the necessary tools to benefit from positive Chi.   You will be shown how to reduce or eliminate the effects of negative energy.   Once you become aware of the tremendous natural energies touching everyone of us, you can turn this powerful force to your advantage.   A general understanding of Chi is essential in mastering the art of Feng Shui.

Magnetic Fields in the Earth's Crust

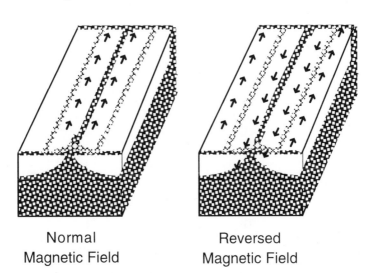

| Normal | Reversed |
| Magnetic Field | Magnetic Field |

Although   the   earth   is   surrounded   by   the magnetosphere, there are also other powerful forces contained in the layers of the earth.   Within the outer layers of the earth, close to the surface, are magnetic fields that reverse themselves over thousands of years. Scientists can observe the movement of these magnetic fields over as short a period as one day.   Modern science can only theorize that the origin of our magnetic energy is attributed to circulating electric currents in the earth's core. The inner core of the Earth is so hot that materials are thought to have no permanent magnetic properties.

MAN'S RELATIONSHIP WITH HIS ENVIRONMENT

With Feng Shui, humans can adjust their surroundings to best suit their environment. Often man imposes himself without much thought to environmental harmony.

For example, in rural China disruption of land caused by excessive plowing, erosion or other processes is believed to disrupt Chi flow. A break in the positive Chi flow would negatively affect those living nearby. The Chi disruption could be bad for your health. Today, living next to a massive construction or excavation project has the same effect.

When man lives in harmony with the environment, a more healthy state is promoted. Living in disharmony disrupts your spiritual, mental and physical health. Disease soon follows.

How is harmony through Feng Shui obtained? We know that disruptions in the Chi flow cause illnesses of various sorts.   This will be further explained in later chapters. For now, know that there are remedies for Chi disruptions. For example, a dark, cold room stagnates and disrupts the Chi flow. Obviously a person living or working in such a room would feel depressed, cold and uncomfortable. Remedies would include installation of windows or artificial lighting to increase light and heat.

Remedy for Dark Rooms

A dark area can be easily fixed
by adding lights or a skylight

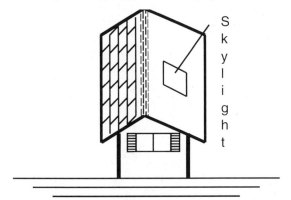

The previous examples of Chi flow disruptions are common examples of man-made negative energy. Not all negative energy is created by polar Chi forces. What happens if a structure is not sited harmoniously? What difference does it make what direction a house faces? The laws of Feng Shui say the direction a structure faces is a significant factor. You can remember from chapter 1 that Feng Shui considers the building, people, environment and timing when evaluating the aspects of a structure.

Decorative ceramic and jade pieces
are used when an earth remedy is needed.

Components of Feng Shui Analysis

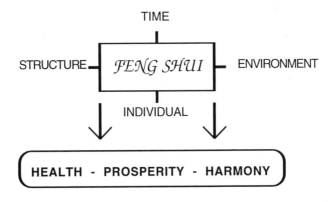

A structure is affected by a specific energy depending on it's facing direction. The Chi force contained within the Earth's polar magnetic fields endows a structure with positive as well as negative energy. The key in Feng Shui analysis is to reside in a home/office with as much positive Chi in the primary living areas.

You will learn in the following chapters that the main entrance, center area of a structure and master bedroom are primary Chi locations. The idea is to maximize positive energy in these key areas and limit negative energy to lower use areas such as the garage, kitchen and storage areas of a home.

A completed building contains a certain energy depending on the year it was built. For example, Feng Shui masters regularly encounter clients who become financially successful. They often are entrepreneurs who started with nothing and amassed a fortune. After several years, they usually want a larger and more luxurious home to match their success. Often, without consulting a Feng Shui master, their move to a more luxurious home is accompanied by an onset of financial or health problems. The change in fortune/health is due to the negative energy affecting the new house. Even identical tract houses built in the same month can be radically different if their directions are different.

A House's Energy Changes with Direction

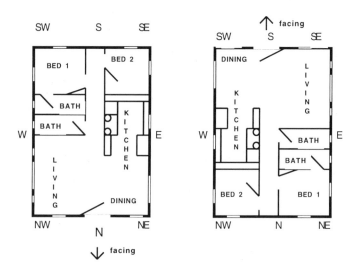

Feng Shui teaches that your living/working environment is in constant change. Changes occur on a daily, weekly, monthly and yearly cycle. With this perpetual change cycle, the effects on you also change. These effects can be negative, positive or a combination of both. The most significant change occurs every twenty years. As explained in chapter one, the magnetic fields change every twenty because of the Saturn/Jupiter conjunction. A house that had energy conducive to financial success or family harmony could radically change in a new twenty year cycle.

20 Year Jupiter/Saturn Earth Cycle

From	1904	1924	1944	1964	1984	2004
To	1923	1943	1963	1983	2003	2023

Your living and working environment are also affected in many subtle as well as obvious ways. The flow of Chi energy can be affected by natural topographical features such as mountains, rivers and valleys. Man-made effects such as high-rise buildings, electrical transformers, and construction sites also shape the Chi flow. For example, a feeling of pressure and unease commonly occurs when living or working in a low-rise building surrounded by high-rise buildings changes.

Pressure Directed onto the Small House

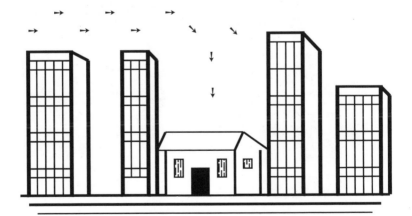

Chi energy is altered and dispersed in a way that negatively affects the inhabitants of the small house. Poor health and bad finances often result from this type of living environment.   Roofing eaves of adjacent structures pointed at your house are another source of negative energy. They can direct negative Chi onto your house.   The negative Chi can negatively impact your health.

This house is overgrown with trees and bushes. Trimming the trees and bushes would eliminate the bad Feng Shui and let in more light.

Man-made structures can often change and disrupt the natural Chi flow.   The Chi, when disrupted, negatively affects the inhabitants of the affected structures.   The ancient masters observed that it was extremely important for man to form a harmonious bond with his environment. Moving against the natural flow of the environment produces negative effects such as ill-health and misfortune.

A decorative brass paperweight
makes a good metal remedy.

SUMMARY

Chi exists in an ever-changing form. Chi energy exists within all living things and permeates our living and working environments. Chi is both negative and positive in nature. Excessive or insufficient Chi affects people negatively, affecting your mental, physical and emotional well-being. A balance of Chi energy is the ideal.

Significant shifts in Chi energy occur every twenty years based on the Saturn/Jupiter alignment. Although Chi changes can be felt in the daily, weekly, monthly and yearly cycles, a dramatic change can occur in structures after a new Jupiter/Saturn shift occurs. The Saturn/Jupiter shift can affect health (mental and physical), finances, relationships and careers significantly.

Man's imposition upon the environment often can cause negative consequences. Chi can be negatively affected by man's altering of the environment. You can use Feng Shui to balance the environment in your favor.

There is a natural order to the universe. When Chi is changed, a cause and effect, either positive or negative can be expected. Nature will always seek to balance the that which is imposed upon the land.

Chapter Three

DISCOVER THE ENERGY FORCES OF THE UNIVERSE

K'an Yu
Historical Chinese name for Feng Shui

Although the energy from Chi, the solar system and earth's magnetic fields form a large part of Feng Shui, there are other important fundamental factors. The understanding of Yin-Yang, the universal law of opposites plays a major role in the remedy and analysis aspects of Feng Shui.

Just as important from the I-Ching are the trigrams. These are an ancient binary-coded system, fundamental to the analysis of Feng Shui. Both ideas remain timeless in their simplicity yet profound in their significance.

YIN-YANG THEORY

The Yin-Yang symbol, seen in many places such as the Korean flag is a fundamental component of the art of Feng Shui. The concept of Yin-Yang has always been seen in China as the basic balancing force of the universe - opposite energies, without which the other could not exist.

Yin-Yang Balance

Yin - Recessive   Yang - Active

For example, Yang symbolizes the day and fire while Yin stands for night and water. Yang is masculine while Yin is feminine. The examples are endless; heat/cold, heaven/earth and night/day. The Yin House of Feng Shui is for the dead, while the Yang House is Feng Shui for the living.

The idea of Yin-Yang is to obtain a balance between two forces. Within Feng Shui, harmonization of Yin and Yang forces produces the most desirable living conditions. Any imbalance can culminate in disease, or misfortune. For example, clients will select a home beneficial for wealth, but detrimental to the owner's health. The master advises the client of the consequences. Nonetheless, the client chooses wealth over health.

Feng Shui masters can attest to large numbers of their clientele who are fabulously wealthy, but suffer from poor health or bad family relations. Feng Shui masters will often counsel their clients to select a house that is harmonious to their health and family relationships, but not as strong financially.

Another way to think of Yin/Yang is to think of a home with excessive light. Obviously, this would cause headaches and general discomfort. During warm weather this house would be uncomfortably warm. A Feng Shui analysis would suggest excessive Yang energy. Architectural changes would be recommended to reduce the sunlight. Modifications could include changing the paint scheme, and tinting or shading the windows.

THE EIGHT TRIGRAMS

For thousands of years the people of China have believed that the eight trigrams of the I-Ching represent the origins of life. Simple in their design, the trigrams are a series of broken and unbroken lines. They are believed to have been sent inscribed on the back of a turtle. The Yin energy is represented by a broken line (- -) and the Yang by a solid line (---).

Each Trigram has a three-part series of lines, therefore, a total of eight different permutations can be formed. You can see from the chart, each trigram is a unique series of three broken or solid lines or a combination.

The 8 Trigrams from the I-Ching

SUN
SOUTHEAST

LI-SOUTH

K'UN
SOUTHWEST

Yang

Yin

TUI WEST

CHEN EAST

CENTER
EARTH

KEN
NORTHEAST

KAN-NORTH

CHIEN
NORTHWEST

Specifically, each trigram contains unique properties and characteristics. The trigrams form a basis for analysis as we shall see later in this chapter. The eight trigrams break down into two main groups. Within the East group are the trigrams; Li, Sun, Kan and Chen. The other group, known as the West contains; Kun, Tui, Ken and Chien. Each trigram is different in the use of broken and unbroken lines. The binary format of each trigram line represents the same data structure of modern computers.

The meaning of each trigram is defined in the later versions of the I-Ching as interpreted by Confucius. The I-Ching provides practical wisdom and divination through the trigrams. The belief, imparted through the I-Ching that change is eternal, provides a logical method by which to analyze cycles of change.

The eight Trigrams as you can see on the preceding chart form an eight-sided shape also known as a Ba-Gua. The Ba-Gua is graphed in a rectangle form for easier analysis. The traditional shape of the Ba-Gua is round. Notice in the rectangularly shaped Ba-Gua that the directions are reversed compared to a normal western compass. The reversal of the compass is a result of the practice of siting a structure. As you can see in the following illustration, a siting has a facing and a sitting position. Normally, the sitting and facing directions are used in a Feng Shui reading.

Sitting and Facing Positions

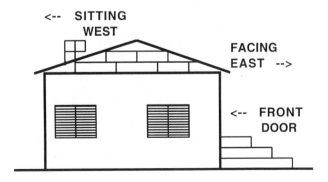

The facing direction is found by looking out from the door frame. The sitting direction is the opposite of the facing direction.

In later chapters you will learn how to superimpose the **Ba-Gua** (Trigram) over structures such as houses and office s.). The analysis resulting from the **Ba-Gua** superimposition will tell much about the positive or negative qualities of your environment.

Master Sang lecturing on the trigrams at the American Feng Shui Institute.

Ba-Gua   (Trigrams)

a aggressiveness adventure

Flexible progressive

persistance calm dependable supportive nurturing

SE	S	SW
SUN	LI	K'UN
WOOD	FIRE	EARTH
4	9	2
E	CENTER	W
CHEN	EARTH	TUI
WOOD	5	METAL
3		7
NE	N	NW
KEN	K'AN	CHIEN
EARTH	WATER	METAL
8	1	6

Celebrity temperimental inflexible

Lively talkative abrasive

Stubborn resist change dependable

president to the point

intuitive flexible

Each trigram represents many things including; direction, element (discussed in the next chapter) and a number. Every trigram rules different parts of the body. Traditionally, each trigram is associated with a family member. The trigram is useful for determining illnesses and provides a specific cure based on the trigram's ruling element.

For example, if an earth energy was negatively dominating a water element, a metal remedy would be prescribed to reduce the dominating (negative) influence of the earth energy. In Feng Shui analysis, energies affect each other in pairs as explained in Yin-Yang theory.

The combining of two energies can be complimentary, or negative with one dominating the other. One trigram can also reduce the power of another trigram. Let us see what role each trigram plays by analyzing their specific qualities.

CHIEN

Trigram:

Symbology:	Heaven
Associated Element:	Metal
Direction:	Northwest
Associated Number:	6
Associated Body Parts	Head, Lungs
Bodily illnesses:	Headaches, Pulmonary Diseases, Fever
Human Associations:	Father, Husband, President, Owner
Trigram Group:	West

The Chien trigram is distinguished by the three solid lines in it's trigram. In the practice of Feng Shui, a trigram will enable a master to determine qualities, problems, and benefits depending on a particular situation.

For example, a part of a home with a west facing direction could suggest headaches or other medical problems associated with Chien for the inhabitant of that room. Of course many other factors as we shall learn later in this book would aid in your diagnosis. In addition, within the practice of Feng Shui, people are associated with a specific trigram. For example, a Chien person (as determined by your birthday) often has the qualities of a metal-like persona such as "to the point" (blunt). He/she is a leader and the head of household.

Chien rules the pulmonary and neurological regions of the body. You may have problems in these areas under certain circumstances explained later. For example, the energy in a Chien facing room may show problems in the head or lungs under certain conditions.

Chien is associated with the number 6. Numbers themselves take on a meaning and are used to reference the Chien Trigram as explained in later chapters.

The sharp edge of this building would be considered metal energy. You could reduce the negative influence by placing a fish tank near the point in your home where the corner is directed.

K'UN

Trigram:

Symbology:	The Earth
Associated Element:	Earth
Direction:	Southwest
Associated Number:	2
Associated Body Parts	Abdomen, Stomach
Bodily illnesses:	Digestive Disorders
Human Associations:	Mother, Wife,
	Old Woman
Trigram Group:	West

The Kun Trigram is represented by three broken lines. As you can see, Kun is the opposite of Chien's three solid lines. It represents mother, wife and elderly women.

Medical disorders are common in the abdominal area with implications such as digestive problems, obstetrical difficulties, gastro-intestinal diseases and other anomalies associated with the abdominal region of the body.

Kun is associated with number 2 and has been traditionally a west direction. The number itself is neither negative nor positive but is representative of Kun qualities as a whole. Kun is an earthly quality, giving a person such traits as persistence, dependability and a calm demeanor. They also can be nurturing and supportive. This Trigram is associated with the West Group. It is thought of as Yang in nature.

CHEN

Trigram:

Symbology:	Thunder
Associated Element:	Wood
Direction:	East
Associated Number:	3
Associated Body Part:	Feet, Throat, Neck
Bodily illnesses:	Convulsions, Hysteria, Anxiety
Human Associations:	Eldest Son, Royalty, Celebrity Status
Trigram Group:	East

Chen can be identified by it's first two broken lines and single solid line. This Trigram is identified with the East Group making it Yin in nature and identified with the number three.

Medical difficulties commonly associated with Chen include hysterical behavior, fits, convulsions, anxiety and podiatric complications such as flat feet, in-grown toenails and swelling. Other problems are associated with the neck such as throat disorders and "stiff neck". Chen shows a strong association with the eldest son, personal fame and celebrity status. Chen symbolizes thunder and is a wood element. It should be noted that the character of the wood is hard and strong such as oak. Personal attributes common to Chen are temperamental, magnetic, inflexible and charismatic.

SUN

Trigram:

Symbology:	Wind
Associated Element:	Wood
Direction:	Southeast
Associated Number:	4
Associated Body Parts	Thighs, Buttocks
Bodily illnesses:	Colds, Rheumatism
Human Associations:	Eldest Daughter, Traveller
Trigram Group:	East

The Sun Trigram has two solid lines and a third broken line. Sun is symbolized by "wind" and is from the East Group making it Yin in nature. A southeast direction is associated with Sun.

Although Sun rules the thighs and buttocks parts of the body, illnesses relating to colds, rheumatism and other viruses are common. Sun is a wood element, but it is thought of as a "softer" wood such as balsawood.

Personality traits associated with Sun include flexibility, malleable, indecisive and progressive. This Trigram rules the eldest daughter, travellers, and number 4.

K'AN

Trigram:

Symbology:	Water
Associated Element:	Water
Direction:	North
Associated Number:	One
Associated Body Parts	Kidneys, Ears, Blood
Bodily illnesses:	Kidney Diseases, Ear Disorders
Human Associations:	Second Son, Middle-aged men
Trigram Group:	East

Kan is an East Group Trigram making it primarily Yin in nature. Associated with the second son and middle-aged people, Kan personalities can be anxious, moody and have a strong "feeling" and intuitive nature. Flexibility is also an attribute of this sign. Diseases of this Trigram include ear and kidney disorders in addition to mood changes and anxiety.

A north direction is assigned to Kan with the number 1. As a water Trigram, Kan also can be changeable. A stream alternating between straight and crooked is a common Chinese analogy for Kan. Just like water in a cup, Kan conforms to it's environment.

LI

Trigram:	▬▬▬▬▬▬▬▬
	▬▬▬ ▬▬▬
	▬▬▬▬▬▬▬▬

Symbology:	Fire
Associated Element:	Fire
Direction:	South
Associated Number:	9
Associated Body Parts:	Eyes, Heart
Bodily illnesses:	Eye, Heart and Circulatory
Human Associations:	Second Daughter, Middle-aged Women
Trigram Group:	East

Li is very dynamic and associated with the East Group making it Yin in nature. The Li's strong nature is a result of it's association with the sun and fire. Li traits often include rash behavior, aggressiveness, and an adventurous streak. Arguments are common with Li energy.

Number nine belongs to Li. Known medical anomalies include a whole range of eye disorders, heart disease, circulatory dysfunctions such as arteriosclerosis and other related disorders.

Li also symbolizes the second daughter and middle-aged women. It's direction is southerly.

KEN

Trigram:

Symbology:	Mountains
Associated Element:	Earth
Direction:	Northeast
Associated Number:	8
Associated Body Parts	Hands, Fingers
Bodily illnesses:	Arthritis, Finger Problems
Human Associations:	Youngest Son, Youth
Trigram Group:	West

Because of it's association with mountains, Ken has a stubborn and unyielding streak. It's other traits include dependability, steadfastness and resistance to change. Ken is a member of the West Group making it Yang in nature.

Medical disorders suggest arthritic dysfunctions, broken fingers and related problems such as Carpal Tunnel Syndrome. Ken is associated with number 8, the youngest son and youth in general. It is also an earth element and northeast in direction.

TUI

Trigram:

Symbology:	Marshes
Associated Element:	Metal
Direction:	West
Associated Number:	7
Associated Body Parts:	Chest, Mouth, Teeth
Bodily illnesses:	Oral/Dental, Thorax disorders
Human Associations:	Youngest Daughter, Young women
Trigram Group:	West

The Tui trigram is associated with marshes and with metal. Personality traits include liveliness, talkative, abrasiveness and nervousness. The number 7 and west direction are uniquely Tui. It is part of the West Group making it primarily Yang in nature.

Medical problems include common dental/oral diseases and chest disorders. Tui is identified with the youngest daughter and young women. The metal of Tui is considered more malleable and softer then Li. Therefore, the nature of Tui is the softer of the two metal trigrams.

PRACTICE EXERCISES

Use the following examples to verify your knowledge of this chapter's material. If you feel confused in the slightest, read this chapter again before doing the practice exercise.

Fill in the blanks on the following chart:

TRIGRAM	DIRECTION	NUMBER	ELEMENT
Chien	_NW_	6	Metal
K'un	Southwest	2	Earth
Chen	E	3	WooD
Sun	Southeast	4	Wood
K'an	N	1	Water
Li	South	9	Fire
KEN	NE	8	EArth
Tui	West	7	metal

Answers can be found in the answer appendix.

SUMMARY

A Feng Shui master uses the Ba-Gua (Eight Trigrams) as his base analytical tool. Think of them as the instrument gauges of a high performance jet plane. Each Trigram is like a gauge giving a specific answer to a specific part of the plane. A sound knowledge of the Eight Trigrams are necessary for any Feng Shui analysis. It's recommended that you review this section several times.

In summary form below is a chart of the Eight Trigrams and their characteristics to be used for review.

Trigram   Meaning

Trigram	Element	Number	Direction	Body	Group
Chien	Metal	6	North west	Head, Lung	West
Kun	Earth	2	South west	Abdo-men	West
Chen	Wood	3	East	Feet, Throat	East
Sun	Wood	4	South east	Thigh	East
Kan	Water	1	North	Ear, Kidney	East
Li	Fire	9	South	Eye, Heart	East
Ken	Earth	8	North east	Hands	West
Tui	Metal	7	West	Mouth, Chest	West

An earth remedy such as a ceramic vase can be decorative and effective. In traditional Feng Shui, an earth remedy would be used to remedy excess fire energy. The plant, signifying wood would be used to strengthen the personal wood trigram of the owner.

This house would be considered bad Feng Shui. It's surrounded on all 4 sides by multi-story apartments. A negative sense of pressure would be felt by the owners of this house.

Chapter Four

PUT CHI POWER TO WORK FOR YOU

The Five Natural Elements

Our living environment consists of many different things. We have furniture, fish tanks, televisions, vases and the like. All of the items are just some of the things that we place into our homes. These things are part of our living and working spaces. Feng Shui classifies all parts of our environment into one of five essential elements.

This classification system includes the elements; wood, fire, earth, metal and water. Everything within our world can be placed somewhere in this file system. For example, a beautiful indoor fichus plant would be part of the wood group. Ceramic vases, made from clay would be considered earth. An aquarium would be considered part of the water group. A brass figurine would be part of the metal group. A red painting or tapestry would be considered part of the fire group. A fireplace would be classified in the fire group only if it burned continuously.

TRADITIONAL FIVE ELEMENTS

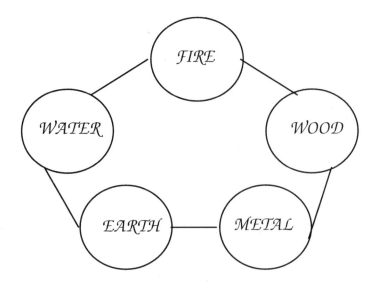

Examples of the Five Elements

Water	Fire	Earth	Wood	Metal
Aquarium	Red tapestry	Vases	Indoor plants	brass statues
fountain		Clay Figurines		cuckoo clocks
				metal blinds

Why are the five elements important? What role does this system play in Feng Shui? All five elements represents a different energy. How these energies interact with each other form one of the most important aspects of Feng Shui. Certain elements are harmonious with each other, others clash, dominate or weaken the other.

So, how does this affect me? How does Feng Shui incorporate the elements into an analytical form? We know that different energies are present in different areas of any structure. The energies can be categorized into one of the five elements. That is, the Chi energy in a specific area has an elemental quality. This energy can be beneficial or detrimental to the person occupying the premises.

For example, in a real life case, a woman developed severe pain and swelling in her left knee. She visited several Los Angeles area orthopedic specialists who could not find a diagnosis. They could only prescribe pain-killers to aid her condition. After three years of unsuccessful treatment, the woman consulted Master Sang. The master determined that her condition appeared after a move to a new home. Excessive metal energy was discovered in her bedroom. This specific type of metal energy commonly affects the legs. As explained in Yin/Yang theory, there are two counter-balancing energies that produce positive energy properly balanced.

Metal energy overpowered the wood energy that was present. Because wood rules the feet and lower extremities the imbalance appeared in persistent knee problems. The master advised placement of an aquarium in her bedroom to balance the metal energy with the wood energy. She has since experienced complete relief from her knee pain and has completely eliminated the pain pills she took for three years.

Let us first examine the five elements and then show how they affect each other. Finally, we will discuss the remedies for elemental imbalances. Again, a thorough understanding of the five elements is essential to the study of Feng Shui. Review this chapter several times to obtain the most benefit.

WOOD

The element wood traditionally consists of live plants and trees. At this point, it is important to note that elements are associated with specific numbers, colors. Each element also rules a specific area of the body. The following chart gives the numbers, colors, and affiliated body areas for wood.

Characteristics of Wood

Trigram	Number	Color	Body Association
Chen	3	Green	Feet, Throat
Sun	4	Green	Thighs, Buttocks

For every energy force present in a given environment there is a counter-energy. For purposes of analysis, a Feng Shui master examines the two energies present and suggests a remedy based on the interactions of the two energies. For example, persistent sore throats may suggest that the Chen/wood energy in your bedroom may be suppressed by a metal energy.

It is also important to note that colors, numbers and certain areas of the body associate with the wood group and possess "wood-like" energy. For wood, there are two different wood trigrams. Chen energy is a harder and stronger wood compared to the lighter and softer Sun version.

The color green, whether worn as clothing or used to decorate your home or office gives the wearer or structure with wood energy. However, color has the weakest effect as a remedy. The actual element should be introduced for the most powerful effect. When an imbalance occurs with wood elements, a person can expect those medical problems associated with the wood group.

WATER

The Water element is of course associated with anything aquatic in nature. The water element could be represented by a swimming pool, aquariums, water fountains or being close to a lake, river, stream or ocean.

Characteristics of Water

Trigram	Number	Color	Body Association
K'an	1	Blue, Black	Ears, Blood, Kidney

The colors, blue and black are associated with water. A person wearing these colors or a room decorated with these colors express water qualities. A deficiency of water energy caused by another over-riding element can cause ear and kidney problems for a person.

FIRE

The Fire element is of a hot nature represented not only by actual fire but also by the color red. An imbalance and weakening of Fire by another element can result in eye or heart complications.

Characteristics of Fire

Trigram	Number	Color	Body Association
Li	9	Red	Eyes, Heart

EARTH

The element Earth is represented by the numbers 2, 5, and 8. Colors associated with Earth include Yellow, Tan and Beige. The element Earth can be associated with clay pottery and statues.

Also considered earthly in nature are non-metallic minerals such as marble art pieces, quartz rocks and any other kinds of natural rocks and boulders. Living close to large mountains will give you a powerful earth energy.

Characteristics of Earth

Trigram	Number	Color	Body Association
K'un	2, 5	Beige, Tan, Yellow	Abdomen, Stomach
Ken	8	Beige, Tan, Yellow	Hands, Fingers

A deficiency of Earth energy caused by another dominating element can include arthritis, hand problems, and complications of the digestive tract.

METAL

All things made from metal such as brass figurines, silver and gold jewelry are metal in nature. Also considered to be metal in nature are grandfather clocks.

Characteristics of Metal

Trigram	Number	Color	Body Association
Chien	6	White, Gold	Head, Lung
Tui	7	White, Gold	Mouth, Chest

Medical problems associated with diminished metal energy include oral disorders, pulmonary disease and chest-area complications.

We have briefly covered the five elements and you should have a general understanding of how an object, color or disease is classified by element. In the next part of this chapter, we will see how the elements interact, dominate, nourish and weaken each other.

HOW THE 5 ELEMENTS INTERACT

We have examined how each of the five elements differ in color, body association, diseases and number. This part of the chapter will discuss how the five elements affect each other.

Within Feng Shui, the five elements interact in a process called "cycles". There are three cycles called; the Productive Cycle, the Domination Cycle and the Reductive Cycle. Think of the "cycle" analysis in terms of a Yin/Yang relationship. There are two energies or "forces" that interact with each other. The relationship between the two energies can be negative, neutral or positive depending on the combination.

However, don't fall into the trap of thinking that the relationship of two energies can be completely negative or positive. For example, Two energies can produce many wealth opportunities. But, your relationships or health may suffer. Or, a particular combination may produce peaceful and tranquil family relationships, but your career potential may not be as strong as it could be. You may already be thinking about creating a nice balance between harmony, health and wealth? Maybe peace and happiness is more important to you than riches. Read on and create the environment you want and deserve.

A particular element will nourish another that is positive in nature. Another element will prevail over or dominate another. This creates an imbalance as one energy dominates at the expense of the other. This results in negative and unhealthful consequences. Lastly, there is a reductive cycle that serves to "lessen" a dominating energy. The reductive cycle is used for remedies and is considered neutral. We will examine each cycle and how it fits into Feng Shui analysis.

THE PRODUCTIVE CYCLE OF
THE FIVE ELEMENTS

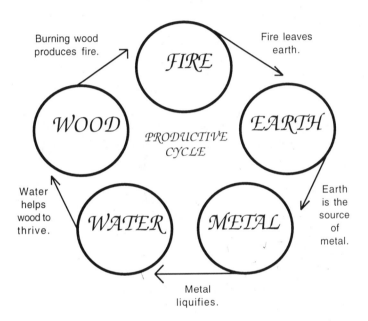

The Productive Cycle shows how one element can "nourish" or "help" another element. For example, the water element helps the wood element to thrive. You can see from the previous illustration that every element has a corresponding element that "nourishes" it.

The Productive Cycle is positive in nature. That is, those elements in a productive relationship are balanced and produce positive effects. The energy from a productive cycle relationship can be in a relationship between two people or in the bedroom of your house. If energies are not in balance as in the productive cycle, you commonly get illness, disease and misfortune. Often times a productive remedy is introduced to strengthen the personal trigram of the owner.

THE DOMINATION CYCLE OF
THE FIVE ELEMENTS

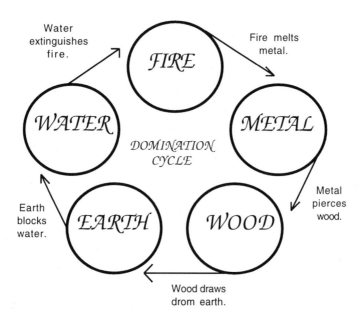

Water extinguishes fire.

Fire melts metal.

WATER

FIRE

METAL

DOMINATION CYCLE

Metal pierces wood.

Earth blocks water.

EARTH

WOOD

Wood draws drom earth.

The Domination Cycle shows which element dominates or overpowers another element. For example, from the chart you can see that fire dominates metal. That is, the heat of the fire melts metal. When metal and fire elements interact an imbalance occurs. Because one element overpowers another, the resulting imbalance is negative.

When an element dominates another, such as metal by fire, a person could experience medical problems associated with to that metal trigram. Remember that each of the trigrams has an element associated with it. Each trigram, when dominated by another trigram, will manifest itself in ways unique to that trigram.

THE REDUCTIVE CYCLE OF
THE FIVE ELEMENTS

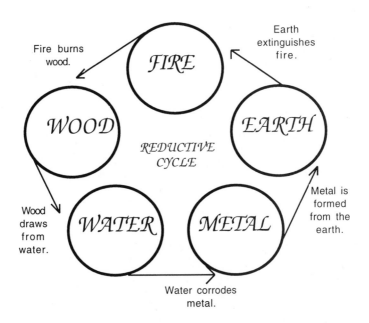

The last cycle is the Reductive. It is used to remedy imbalances created by the domination cycle. For example, with fire and metal elements, fire will dominate metal. An imbalance occurs. Using the Reductive Cycle illustrated above, the introduction of earth into the environment "reduces" the strength of fire. Another example of reduction is the wood-fire relationship. Fire can burn wood to ashes, therefore it weakens the property of wood. Thus, using the reductive cycle reduces the strength of the dominating element. A reductive relationship is considered neutral.

The reduction corrects the dominating imbalance. Using a fire/metal combination you can see from the Reductive Cycle that you would introduce earth to reduce the dominating power of fire over metal. How is this done? You can recall from earlier in the chapter that the earth element includes porcelain and clay figures. Beige, tan and yellow colors also have an earth energy.

The master would suggest that if this imbalance was at the entrance, large rocks of a decorative nature or large clay pottery should be placed near the entrance. In a bedroom you could place tasteful vases to offset the imbalance.

Decorative vases (earth) can be used to reduce the energy of excessive fire.

Please note that when using the Reductive Cycle to reduce the influence of an element, you must be very careful. Introducing an incorrect element can have a powerful effect. Review the cycles as often as needed until you feel comfortable with this knowledge.

In a remedy situation using the reductive cycle, it is always advisable to introduce the actual element. The elemental color may be introduced if the placing of an object is not possible. Still, color is not as powerful a remedy as an object made from the reducing element. Sometimes, such as when using fire to reduce wood, only use of the color is possible. An actual fire is not usually practical since it must be continually burning to be effective. When using color to reduce you can use art prints that contain the color, tapestries, or even paint the walls or replace the carpeting with the reductive color. Combining color and the actual element in your remedies strengthen the remedy.

Decorative indoor plants can be used when you need a wood reducer.

Remember that if you use fire as a remedy, the flame must be continuously burning. You may also use the color red by itself (which is not as effective).

This is a nice residential street, except that it backs up against high-rises. These condominiums are overpowered by the adjacent office building. In addition, the Feng Shui of the building is reversed by the high-rise and could create negative energy.

Fish tanks are an excellent water remedy. Please remember to change the water and clean the tank regularly for best results. To enhance your luck add 6 fish or place 6 coins in the tank. Generally, the larger the tank you use, the more powerful the remedy.

CHAPTER QUIZ
(answers at the bottom of the page)

1.   What element dominates fire? *water*

2.   What element would you use to reduce water? *-Wood*

3.   What element would you use to strengthen *fire*
      and support earth?

4.   A ceramic vase is an example of what element? *earth*

5.   A red tapestry is an example of what element? *Fire*

6.   Indoor plants are an example of which element? *wood*

7.   The a. smaller b. larger c. brighter d. more   *B*
      expensive a remedy is, the more powerful it
      becomes.

8.   Earth is used to reduce what element? *Fire*

9.   If you wanted to strengthen metal what element *wood*
      would you use?

10.   Introducing fire would dominate what element? *metal.*

Answers to the above

1. Water   2. Wood
3. Fire   4. Earth
5. Fire   6. Wood
7. Larger 8. Fire
9. Wood   10. Metal

SUMMARY

All things may be classified into one of five elements
consisting of fire, water, earth, metal or water. It can be
a color, an article of clothing, or an object made from the
elements. You also will learn further in the book, that
people as well as buildings possess elemental energies.

Elemental Cycles

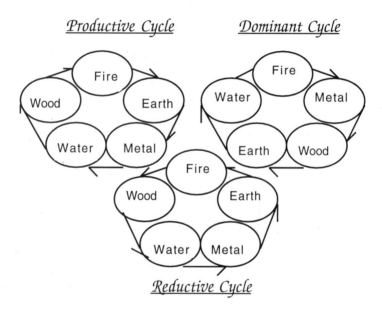

As you've learned, the Productive Cycle is positive in nature.   One element nourishes the other.   The Domination Cycle is negative.   When an energy dominates or exerts control over another element, an imbalance forms.   In the Reductive Cycle, another element can reduce the power of a dominating element and is considered neutral.

Remember that you must be absolutely sure of yourself when introducing a reductive element. It is better not to use the Reductive Cycle at all unless you have thoroughly mastered the knowledge in this chapter. Check the beginning of the chapter to review objects suitable for reduction. Any item listed in the elemental charts provided it is the correct element would be appropriate for use in reduction remedies.

When using the reductive cycle, introduction of an object made from the reducing element is the most effective.   Use of a reducing color will not be as powerful.

There are many decorative pieces that can be used for your remedies. This large metal wall piece makes an excellent metal remedy. Try and choose your remedies with an artistic eye. An unattractive remedy may cause you unease if the piece is displeasing to the eye.

Chapter Five

KNOW YOUR OWN
UNIQUE LIFE-FORCE

CHI
The Universal Energy Force

We briefly considered the individual, environment, time and structure components of Feng Shui. That is, these four factors form the basis for an accurate Feng Shui reading. The importance of the individual factor and your birth year will be discussed in this chapter.

Elements of Feng Shui Analysis

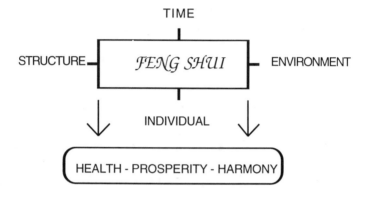

An important aspect of Feng Shui is the a person's birthday in determining the compatibility with a particular property. As you may recall, the energy (Chi) fields that envelop earth change on a daily, monthly, yearly and twenty year cycle. We discussed that the twenty year cycle is the most important to people in terms of major changes. Second in importance is the annual cycle that forms the basis for determining your personal trigram.

The biggest holiday for the Chinese is the Lunar New Year Chinese. It is an opportunity to examine the past year and hope for a more prosperous and happy year. The Chinese New Year begins on February 5 of every year as compared to January 1 for those of us in the west.

A specific energy existed on earth at the time of your birth. This Chi energy, specific to your year of birth, came into you when you inhaled your first breath of life.

Your birth energy may or may not be compatible with your home and office energies. The energy obtained at birth enables you to figure out whether a particular house is compatible with your energy.

More specifically, certain directions are more favorable to you personally than others. In addition, your direction based on your birth year may not be good for another person. For example, if an eastern direction is beneficial for you, a house that sits to the east would be harmonious with your energy. Traditionally, Feng Shui has used the sitting direction of a structure as well as the facing position. Try not to confuse the two positions. Think of the sitting position as the opposite direction of the facing direction.

Sitting Versus Facing Direction

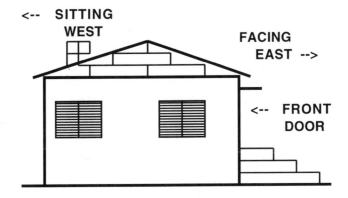

A direction incompatible with your trigram's energy can produce negative effects. For example, if a west direction is unfavorable to you, your luck, health, financial and marital situations could be negatively affected. This chapter also will examine other factors besides direction that come with your trigram.

THE IMPORTANCE OF YOUR
PERSONAL TRIGRAM

In an earlier chapter we reviewed the eight trigrams and their individual qualities. Now we will discuss how the trigrams apply to people. As you can see on the following trigram chart, there are specific names, elements, and numbers associated with each trigram.

Within Feng Shui, every person identifies with a specific trigram based on their birthday. Knowing your trigram is useful in analyzing your relationships. The following chart shows the traditional trigram chart and the qualities they each represent.

Your personal trigram is often used in Feng Shui to identify benefits, problems and physical disorders. For example, a person with a K'un trigram may experience stomach problems caused by his bedroom. The bedroom may also have strong wood energy that dominates the earth energy of K'un.

At this point, just understand that energy exists in pairs. Your own energy interacts with other energies. It can be the energy of your house as a whole, a bedroom of your house or another person.   The energy relationship can be positive, negative or neutral.

Traditional Trigram Layout

SE SUN WOOD 4	S LI FIRE 9	SW K'UN EARTH 2
E CHEN WOOD 3	CENTER EARTH 5	W TUI METAL 7
NE KEN EARTH 8	N K'AN WATER 1	NW CHIEN METAL 6

What other information besides direction does a trigram give to you as a person? How do I use my trigram once I find it? How do I find my trigram? These questions will be answered here and elaborated upon in later chapters.

You will recall from chapter four that the five elements operate within the three cycles of domination, reduction and production. Your trigram will show how you interact with other people based on the three relationship cycles. For example, if you are a Chen person, based on your birthday, you identify with the wood element. If your wife is a K'an person (associated with water), she would be productive to your wood

element.   This signifies a positive, nurturing and
harmonious relationship.

If your supervisor at work is a Tui person (associated
with metal), he would dominate and overshadow you.
The Chen/wood element is dominated by metal. Check
the domination cycle chart to verify. If you have a
friend who is Li (associated with the fire element), this
person would "reduce" your strength and weaken your
personality in a relationship. As you can see from the
reduction cycle, wood is reduced by fire although the
effect would be less powerful than a   dominating
relationship.

Medical disorders associated with a trigram can occur
when the trigram is dominated by specific types of
energy incompatible with your trigram's energy. When
energies are not in harmony, an imbalance occurs. The
imbalance can be manifested through disease, negative
relationships and poor financial conditions. Diseases
will be covered in great detail in the last chapter of this
book.

Reexamine the three cycles below and then move on to
find your trigram. Please note that knowledge of the
elemental cycles is fundamental to a thorough mastery
of Feng Shui. Find the birthdays of important people in
your life and figure out how their energy harmonizes
with you. Look for your relationships in all three cycles.

The 3 Elemental Cycles

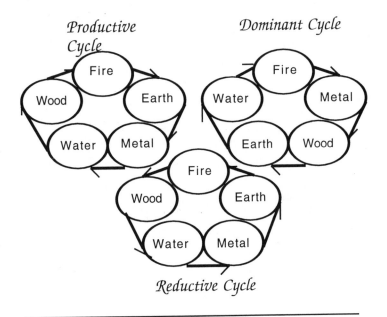

Productive Cycle

Dominant Cycle

Reductive Cycle

Let us now find your particular personal trigram. Then we will analyze the significance of your personal trigram, and how it applies to your living and working environment.

FINDING YOUR PERSONAL TRIGRAM

Note that there are separate formulas for men and women when determining your trigram. It is also advisable to recalculate the trigram formula several times to verify your trigram. Use the trigram formula to calculate the personal trigram for all your relationships. After your calculations, examine your relationships and see if they are dominant, productive or reductive.

Birthday Trigram Formula

Formula for a Male: (100 - year of birth)/9 = X
Use the last 2 digits of your birth year.
Use the remainder of X to find your trigram number.
If you have zero remainder, go to #9 in the birthday
trigram chart.

Example: A male born November 5, 1962

Step 1: Put the last 2 numbers of your birth year into
         the formula.
Step 2: Do the math = (100 - 62) / 9 = 4 remainder 2
Step 3: Go to the Trigram Chart and find "Male #2."
         Remainder 2 Male = K'UN

A male born November 5, 1962 belongs to: **K'UN**

Formula for a Female: (year of birth - 4) / 9 = X
Use the last 2 digits of your birth year.
Use the remainder of X to find your trigram number.
If you have zero remainder, go to #9 in the birthday
trigram chart.

Example: A female born September 26, 1962

Step 1: Put the last 2 numbers of your birth year into
         the formula.
Step 2: Do the math = (62 - 4) / 9 = 6 remainder 4
Step 3: Go to the trigram chart and find Female "#4."
         Remainder 4 Female = SUN

A female born September 26, 1962 belongs to: **SUN**

Use February 5 - February 4 as your year (Chinese year).

Trigram   Number   Chart

Li	Ken	Tui	Chien	Ken	Kun	Sun	Chen	Kun	Kan
9	8	7	6	5	5	4	3	2	1

Female   Male

After calculating your trigram, check appendix B to make sure your calculation was correct. Especially take care to use the correct male/female formula. After obtaining your trigram, get to know as much as you can about your trigram. Once you learn your trigram, go back and learn the other trigrams. Solid knowledge of the trigrams is essential to Feng Shui analysis.

Although using the annual Trigram chart is easier than the calculation method, the formula should be learned by serious students of Feng Shui. Serious students will want to learn the trigram formula to reduce dependence on this book.

YOUR PERSONAL TRIGRAM

Fill in the following personal information for your later use:

My trigram is: _SUN_

My color(s) is: _Green_

My element is: _WOOD_

My best direction for relationships is: _EST_

My best direction for wealth is: _____

My body areas are: _____

My trigram is productive to: _____

The trigram productive to mine is: _____

The trigram that I dominate is: _____

The trigram that dominates me is: _____

The trigram I reduce is: _____

The trigram that reduces me is: _____

Congratulations, at this point you should have obtained your personal trigram. Review your trigram information several times. Go back and review any of the meanings and interpretations of your trigram. Those of you seriously pursuing mastery of Feng Shui should know this information completely. Take a few extra minutes and calculate the trigram of your family and friends.

After you have calculated the trigrams of those people important in your life, take a moment and think about the role they play, and how they interact with you. Go back after your reflective analysis and see where in the three cycles they fit in relation to your element.

Human Relationships within the Three Cycles

	Dominant	Productive	Reductive
Example:	Earth over water	wood to fire	earth reduces fire
Effect:	Negative*	Positive**	Neutral***

*The trigram being dominated is negatively affected.

**One element supports another in a positive manner. Any two elements not related in a cycle produces a neutral effect in a relationship.

***The element being reduced is weakened. A reductive relationship does not produce negative results. For example, a Chen person may not want to introduce fire. Fire would reduce the strength of the Chen's wood energy.

A decorative brass globe and jade turtles. The jade (earth) would support the metal in the productive cycle. Metal qualities would dominate because metal also reduces the power of earth in the reductive cycle.

SUMMARY

Follow these steps:

1. Use the trigram formula to find your personal trigram.

2. Double-check using the annual trigram chart.

3. Always use the formula if your are serious about mastering Feng Shui.

4. Examine the qualities of your personal trigram from the Eight-Trigram chart. Many personal qualities will apply to you.

5. Examine carefully the elemental cycles. Analyze which elements affect you in a positive, negative or neutral manner.

6. Figure out the trigrams of those persons important in your life and see how they relate to you within the three cycles.

These are not high-tension wires, however, the transformer is less than 7 feet from this apartment.   The Chinese have observed for many years that electro-magnetism often causes disease and misfortune.

Chapter Six

PINPOINT YOUR BEST LIVING
AND WORKING SPACE

EARTH ELEMENT

This chapter will enable you to accurately site your home/office. An accurate siting is a critical first step when reading a structure. Your knowledge of Feng Shui theory may be superb, but, a wrong compass siting will invalidate your reading.

How do you take a compass siting? Why is an accurate siting important? How accurate does my siting need to be? How do I site my particular house (which isn't like any of the examples in the book)?   These questions will be addressed in this chapter.   Again, quickly scan the chapter to familiarize yourself with the new information. Go back a second time and **slowly** read the entire chapter again. Review parts of the chapter that don't make sense and keep a dictionary handy if you feel the need.

USING A LO-PAN

The   Chinese have traditionally used a Lo-Pan (compass) to accurately determine the siting of a structure. The Lo-Pan works in the same manner as a conventional compass showing earth's magnetic North and South Poles.

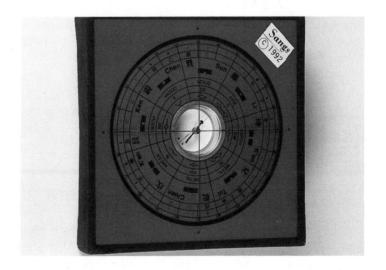

An English Lo-Pan translated by Master Sang.

A conventional map compass may be used if it can measure a full 360 degrees. You can find an appropriate compass in most sporting goods stores. Spend for the highest quality compass you can find. A standard western compass usually doesn't provide an accurate enough reading nor does it contain the markings used in advanced Feng Shui analysis.

We strongly recommend that you purchase a Chinese Lo-Pan compass. The authors, through the non-profit American Feng Shui Society, can provide the readers of this book with a Lo-Pan. It is the only Lo-Pan compass accurately translated into English. See the ordering information at the end of the book for further information.

A correct siting involves measuring two key directions. A Feng Shui master reads both a **facing** and **sitting** direction. For example, if the front door of your house faces to the east, then your house sits to the west. If your front door faces to the northeast, then your sitting position would be to the southwest. Use the following chart to interpret your home.

FACING versus SITTING Chart

A house that:
faces north, sits south
faces west, sits east
faces northwest, sits southeast
faces northeast, sits southwest
faces south, sits north
faces east, sits west
faces southeast, faces northwest
faces southwest, faces northeast

EXAMPLE

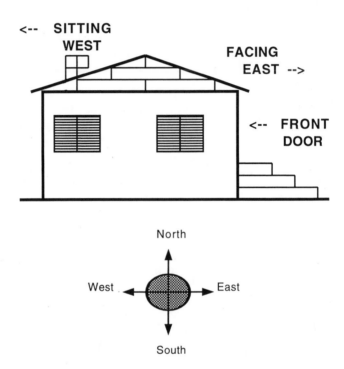

In this example, the front door of the house faces out to the east. The sitting position is the opposite of the facing position. Therefore, the sitting position is west.

Remember to take several compass readings to verify your sitting and facing positions. Stand clear of the door frame and away from any metal objects including watches and jewelry.

PRACTICE EXERCISE

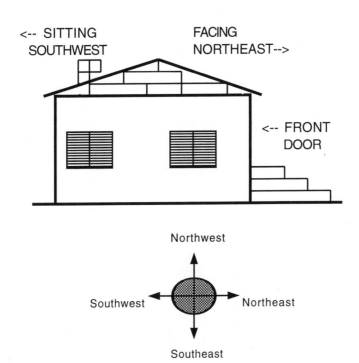

<-- SITTING
SOUTHWEST

FACING
NORTHEAST-->

<-- FRONT
DOOR

Northwest

Southwest   Northeast

Southeast

1. What is the facing direction?

2. What is the sitting direction?

You can find the answers in the appendix.

USING A LO-PAN COMPASS

The correct siting with a Lo-Pan is a simple procedure. Use the following steps and you can rest assured that your compass reading will always be accurate.

1.   Remove your wristwatch and any other heavy jewelry before taking a compass reading. A Lo-Pan is a sensitive instrument easily affected by other magnetic/metal objects.

2.   Try to take your reading at least ten feet from the doorway. Make sure you are not next to a parked car or other metal objects that might affect your reading. Doorways are notorious for affecting Lo-Pans because of their metal content.

3.   Your reading should be taken approximately ten feet in front of the main entrance. You will usually obtain a different reading if you are standing in the doorway.

4.   Face outward with your back to the front door. Align yourself outward, flush with the door. Even a slight deviation will cause a faulty reading.

5.   Look directly over the compass thread. Rotate the compass dial until the needle end with the small circle is lying exactly between the two red dots (Chinese compass only). This gives you your facing direction. The facing direction is always the outward from the front door. The sitting direction is the inward direction of the front door or the opposite of the facing direction.

6.   Finally, take several other readings from other positions. This will verify the accuracy of your Lo-Pan reading.

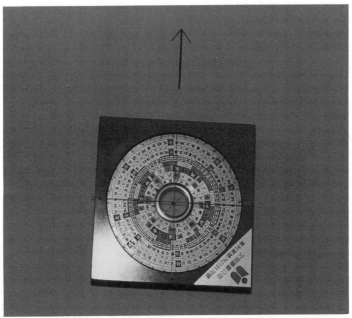

The arrow points to the facing direction (SE).

THE EIGHT ORIENTATIONS

We have by this time determined your personal trigram based on your birthday.   Your personal trigram is useful in analyzing your relationships with other people. At this point we will examine the significance of trigrams when orienting and analyzing your home. You also can use the same procedures to analyze your office.

In Feng Shui the home is more important than your workplace because most people spend more time at home.   Earth's magnetic fields affect the energy in your home. Therefore, the energy within your home affects you in a more powerful manner. Depending upon the positioning of your home, there exists different energy

(Chi) fields within your home. Test this theory yourself. Go to any new home development in your area. Have you noticed that two houses with the same floorplan on similar plots of land "feel" different from each other?

Feng Shui breaks down earth's energies into eight different types consistent with the following trigram chart. Note that the center of the chart represents earth as the center. There is no trigram name or direction for the center trigram quadrant. Remember, when determining the correct trigram for your home use the sitting position. The sitting position of your office is always the opposite of the front door's facing position. Use the following chart to find the correct trigram name for your home or office.

Determining the Trigram of Your Home

Sits	Faces	Trigram
East	West	Chen
West	East	Tui
North	South	K'an
South	North	Li
Northeast	Southwest	Ken
Northwest	Southeast	Chien
Southeast	Northwest	Sun
Southwest	Northeast	K'un

After you have determined your home's trigram name, find your home's actual trigram from the following trigram chart. If your home is a Chen house, choose the one with Chen in the center. If your front door faces south (sits to the north) choose the K'an trigram. Chen and K'an trigrams are part of the East Group. If your front door faces to the east choose Tui (sits to the west). If your door faces to the southwest choose Ken (sits to the northeast). Tui and Ken trigrams are part of the West Group.

East Trigram Group - Direction Rating

	Li	Sun	K'an	Chen
South	D	B	C	A
S-West	F	G	H	E
West	G	F	E	H
N-West	H	E	F	G
North	C	A	D	B
N-East	E	H	G	F
East	A	C	B	D
S-East	B	D	A	C

After you obtain the sitting direction of your house (opposite of the facing position at the front door), you can find the trigram of your home. The above chart will evaluate sections of your home. You can use this process for your workplace as well.

The evaluation of each portion of your home and workplace is based on a lettering system from A to H. At this point, we are concerned only with laying out your home or office floorplan and obtaining an accurate compass reading. Later in this chapter we'll show you how to analyze the different parts of your living and working space. Always take at least 3 compass readings from the front of your house. Remember that metal in the doorways/frame or being close to a car or other large metal object will affect your compass reading. We recommend that you remove your watch before a reading. Double-check with the trigram direction chart to make sure you have the correct trigram for your house.

The rating system, analysis techniques, floorplan layout procedures and remedies will be explained later in this and subsequent chapters. Still, a good analysis always begins with an accurate compass reading. The best analysis is wasted on an inaccurate compass siting.

West Trigram Group - Direction Rating

	Kun	Tui	Ken	Chien
South	F	G	E	H
S-West	D	B	A	C
West	B	D	C	A
N-West	C	A	B	D
North	H	E	G	F
N-East	A	C	D	G
East	E	H	F	B
S-East	G	F	H	E

At this point you can find the trigram of your home. Use the following exercises to practice siting. It's advisable to choose a house that matches your personal trigram. If you cannot find a home that matches your personal trigram, choose a house that is from the same group as your personal trigram. Generally, the house's trigram is more important than your personal trigram. For example, a Chen person should choose a Chen house. If a Chen house is not available, try to find a home from the "East Group" (Li, K'an or Sun).

PRACTICE EXERCISES

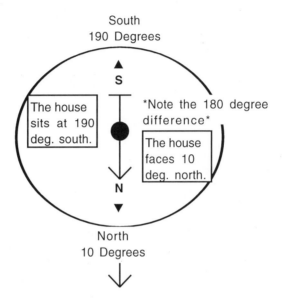

1. Use the compass pictured above. This is the facing
    direction of a house. What is the trigram?

2. A house sits at 60 degrees (Use your compass).
    What is the trigram?

3. My home faces to the: _____

4. My home sits to the: _____

5. The trigram of my home is: _____

Answers can be found in the back of the book.

SITING YOUR HOME AND WORKPLACE

At this point you should have the sitting position and trigram for your home. The next step in siting your home is to draw a sketch of your home's floorplan. Be as accurate and true to scale as you can. Of course a copy of the blueprint floorplan would be ideal. Make sure that your floorplan can be written on as we will be drawing over your floorplan. You may want to make additional copies of your home and office floorplans as we will be using them in later chapters.

Following are some examples of how detailed your floorplan should be. **The floorplan should:**

1. Draw your floorplan true to scale.

2. Show all doors and windows.

3. Show appliances such as stove, range and washer/dryer.

4. Show fireplaces, stairs, closets and garage (if attached).

5. Sketch in your swimming pool/spa (if any), power lines/poles, adjacent streets and any other significant environmental factors.

6. Include design elements such as cathedral ceilings, mirrored doors and ceiling fans.

7. If possible, sketch the contours of your lot. Note any hills, gullies and other adjacent structures.

Sample   Floorplan*

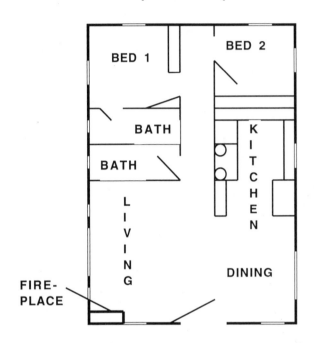

The next step after drawing your floorplan is to design a grid with nine boxes similar to the trigram charts you have seen in previous chapters. Make sure that the grid is proportional and large enough to fit over your particular home. Following is a sample grid drawn for the adjacent floorplan.

*IMPORTANT!

*Include your garage in your analysis if
more than 2/3 is built into the house.

Trigram Grid Should Match the Size of the Floorplan

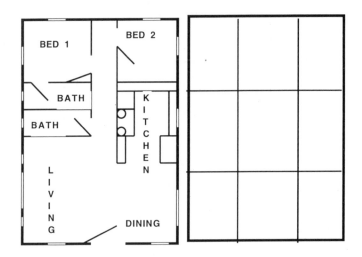

At this point you should have your blank grid corresponding to your floorplan and an actual sketch of your home's floorplan. You also have the trigram that corresponds to your home. If your home is a Chen house (sits to the east), choose Chen. The center of the circle will identify each trigram. Fill in the grid you have just completed with the information from your East/West trigram. Take the letters from the East-West Trigram circle and lay them into the grid.

Remember that the trigrams correspond to the Chinese compass. They are the exact opposite of the Western compass. Match up the letters from the trigram to each floorplan grid. There is no letter for the center floorplan grid.

Write the letters into your home's floorplan grid.

SITTING ———————— EAST

NE F KEN	E D CHEN	SE C SUN
N B KAN	*CHEN*	S A LI
NW G CHIEN	W H TUI	SW E KUN

FACING   ↓   WEST

Following is a sample of a trigram with the numbers entered into the grid. Your next step is to superimpose the grid over your floorplan. Many students find it easier to draw a proportional trigram over their floorplan. You will then enter the letters that correspond to the direction.

Make sure that you label your floorplan with their compass directions. For example, you may want to put "east" next to your front door if your door faces to the east. Label the rest of your floorplan with the remaining seven directions. Double-check your directions after you finish. Beginners often get this process wrong. An incorrect direction label will give you a wrong analysis.

Chen Sample Floorplan

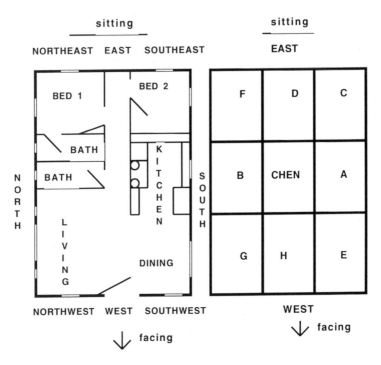

Following is the floorplan with the "Chen" grid superimposed. Some rooms will have two or three different trigrams. If you move your furniture, make sure you are in the part of the room with the desired quadrant.

Chen Floorplan with Grid and Labeling

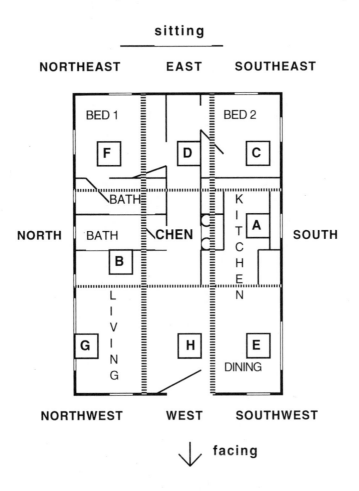

sitting

NORTHEAST   EAST   SOUTHEAST

BED 1   BED 2

F   D   C

BATH

NORTH   BATH   CHEN   KITCHEN   A   SOUTH

B

LIVING   DINING

G   H   E

NORTHWEST   WEST   SOUTHWEST

↓ facing

After you complete the practice exercises, we will move on to the analysis of your floorplan. Beginners usually need practice gridding floorplans. East-West analysis is simple and straightforward. An accurate floorplan and grid is necessary for an accurate Feng Shui analysis. Your analysis may be brilliant, but an imprecise floorplan or labeling can ruin all your work.

PRACTICE EXERCISES

Example #1   Lay in the letters A-H for this house.
Use the Li chart from the East Group trigram chart.

Li Practice Floorplan

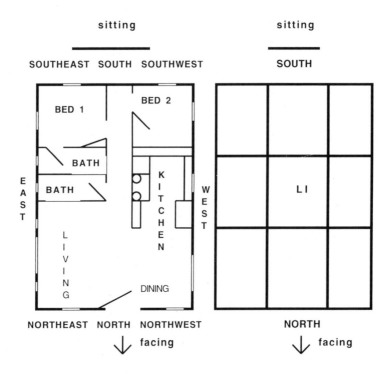

Example #2   Lay in the letters A - H for this Tui office. Use the Tui chart from the West Group trigram chart.

Tui Practice Office Floorplan

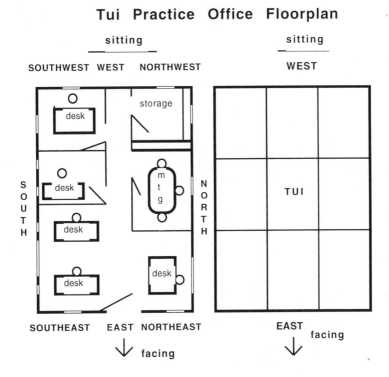

Answers can be found at the end of the book.

EAST-WEST ANALYSIS

You should have sketched your floorplan, and superimposed the trigram grid with the corresponding letters.   At this point we will begin to analyze your floorplan and discuss the meaning and interpretation as pertains to you.   Remember we are using the house trigram. The personal trigram also can be used, but is less significant than the house trigram. Ideally, the personal and house trigram should match.

Let me emphasize that accuracy in siting your home is probably the most important facet of Feng Shui for beginners. Your knowledge of Feng Shui theory may be excellent, but unless your siting is accurate your analysis probably will be completely wrong. Often times it's helpful to have a friend take a compass reading of your home. By getting a concurring second opinion will boost your confidence and help reduce any basic mistakes.

East/West analysis is your first step in analyzing your home or workplace. This forms the basic analysis and is the first level by which we judge the Feng Shui of a structure. In following chapters you will be taught more complex and powerful analysis and remedy tools to use. Still, your East/West analysis provides a good solid basic analysis of your home.

As you examine the following chart, have your floorplan next to you. You will notice that East/West analysis is based on an 8-letter system from A to H. The most important aspect of your East/West analysis is to examine your floorplan and find the best locations.

For example, having a letter "A" at your entrance is a strong, positive energy force portending good fortune and fame. Look at your bedroom. What letter is present there? Optimally, having a letter "D" in the bedroom is good for family harmony and peace.

The letter system runs from "A"- excellent to "H"- worst position. Frequently, a room will have two different quadrants/letters. Use the quadrant where you spend most of your time. In a bedroom it would be where your head lies. Arrange your living space to maximize positive living space. You also can divide each room into trigram quadrants. Use the best quadrants of each room as well. The following analysis chart simplifies your analysis.

East-West Trigram Analysis Chart

EVALUATION	RATING		ANALYSIS
Best									A.	Fortune & Fame
									B.	Wealth & Friendships
								C.	Family Harmony & Good Public Image
							D.	Peace, Good Management
						E.	Arguments, Potential Lawsuits and Fires
					F.	Misfortune and Bad Influences
				G.	Accidents, Disasters, Bad Influences
Worst				H.	Unproductive Career, Bad Finances and Robberies

We have used our sample Chen floorplan as an example. Follow along with your floorplan. Analyze one quadrant of the trigram grid at a time.

Chen Sample Flooplan

sitting

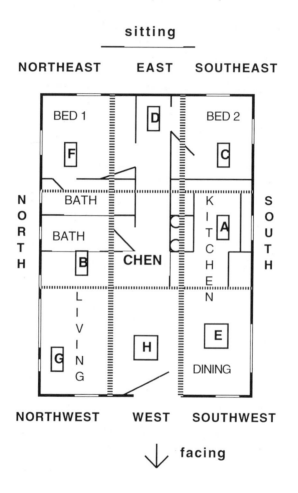

ANALYSIS

Your analysis begins with the front door, master bedroom (bed 1) and the kitchen. This should be your order of analysis. It's also in order of importance. Other rooms can be analyzed after these three.

1. Entrance "H" Position

According to our East-West analysis chart, "H" is the worst position. "H" portends bad career and finances and possibilities of robbery. If your entrance is either E - H, try to use side/back/garage doors located in more favorable quadrants.

2. Master Bedroom "F" and "D" Quadrants

A "F" master bedroom should be avoided. "F" can mean bad luck and evil influences to the owners. The remedy is to move to the second bedroom (C quadrant). If this isn't possible, move the head of your bed against the wall in the "D" quadrant. "D" quadrants are good for family peace and recommended for bedrooms.

3. Kitchen "A" Quadrant

The E - H quadrants should be in the kitchen. The heat from the stove and microwave would burn off the negative energy. Also, kitchens aren't used as much as other rooms such as living/family rooms. A sparsely used room does not affect the owner compared to a heavily used room. In our sample house, the positive qualities of an "A" quadrant are wasted in the kitchen. The positive energy is burned off by the stove.

4. Other Recommendations

Use the "B" part of the living room for your couch, chairs and other furniture that are heavily used.   Try to use as much of the "B" portion of the living room.

You can use bedroom 2 for an office, family room or master bedroom.   It has an excellent "C" and "D" rating.

SUMMARY

Follow these steps:

1. When using a Lo-Pan compass, always take at least two readings from different locations.
Example: Take the first reading near the front door. Take the second reading farther toward the street.

2. Stay at least 20 feet away from metal objects such as cars, doorways, mailboxes etc.
Remove your watch and any other metal jewelry before using the compass.

3. The facing direction of a house is the direction you are facing as you look **OUT** from the front door.

4. The sitting position is always the opposite of the facing position.

5. The **SITTING** direction of your house will tell you which trigram to use in East-West analysis. For example, a house that sits to the east will use the Chen trigram.

6. Double-check your directions and analysis lettering at least twice. Even experienced students make mistakes.

7. Start filling in the East-West with the front door. If the door faces west, write "west" next to the door. The center of the house (trigram) will remain blank.

8. Enter the East-West letter (A-H) for this direction from the trigram.

9. Your entrance and bedroom are the most important areas to analyze. Entrances are areas where energy enters the house. The bedroom is where you spend most of your home time, therefore, the energy in that room will affect you most. The kitchen, bathroom and other low-use areas are best for positions E-H. Heavily used areas are best for letters A-D.

The author and Master Sang, at the
American Feng Shui Institute

Chapter Seven

POWERFUL REMEDIES
TO RELEASE YOUR POTENTIAL

Sha
Chinese Concept of Negative Energy

Until this point, the ideas of Chi and Feng Shui have been examined discussed. That is, we have viewed Chi as beneficial to our general well-being. You can recall in earlier chapters that the Chinese perceive the physical universe in a Yin/Yang duality. Our plane of existence is balanced through two opposing forces. An imbalance or predominance of one force over the other results in disharmony. The disharmony can be manifested in many ways such as illness, misfortune and conflict.

In this chapter we will discuss the results of Chi imbalances and remedies. What are those things that cause discomfort in our living space? Feng Shui gives tools by which to perceive and analyze the negative aspects of our environment.   Feng Shui, can then recommend a remedy. The idea is to balance Yin/Yang energies by reducing the negative and strengthening the positive.

Yin-Yang Balance

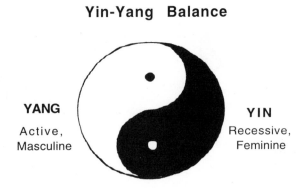

YANG

Active,
Masculine

YIN

Recessive,
Feminine

While Yin and Yang energies are neither positive nor negative. When they are not in balance a negative energy is created. For example, let's say a man has a strong Yang energy. He feels confident that he can run a 26 mile marathon race on a hot day with ease. Halfway through the race, the man has run at 100% of his abilities and succumbs to heat exhaustion. An overabundance of Yang energy can cause internal heat build-up, making a person easily susceptible to heat prostration.

Another example of an imbalance is the design of contemporary homes with wall-sized windows on all sides. These homes are especially popular in California and allow for a panoramic view. The excessive interior sunlight (Yang energy) caused by the windows can be uncomfortable. This is especially true in warm and sunny climates. Strong sunlight can cause headaches and heat build-up in warm weather.

When Yin/Yang imbalances occur within the realm of Feng Shui, we call that condition a Sha. The condition resulting from the windows in the home described above would be called a Sha. A Sha condition is a negative force because of an imbalance and can affect a person in different ways. For example, living in a small 1-story home between tall high-rise buildings increases Sha for the inhabitants of the small house.

Traditional Feng Shui masters believe that the tall buildings cause a pressure on the occupants of the small house. The people who live in the small house between the skyscrapers can be affected through bad health, poor business fortunes or family conflict. Environmental "Sha" imbalances can be manifested through various negative ways on the occupants.

This is just one of the examples of Sha that we will cover in this chapter. In Feng Shui analysis, we would call this an exterior environmental Sha. A Sha also can exist within a home or office as well. We call that an interior Sha. We will discuss the many types of Sha that are common in and outside the home and office and suggest remedies for these conditions.

RECOGNIZING SHA

This section will focus on recognizing Sha energy. If something causes you discomfort, you can label it a Sha. Note that Sha can affect different people in different ways. Often times it can just be a feeling of "pressure" or discomfort. It may or may not be something you can "put your finger on".   Remember that Sha is an imbalance. To remedy the Yin-Yang imbalance, use the suggested methods. These are proven remedies that will help you.

The Feng Shui reading of a home begins with a compass (Lo-Pan) reading. After your first compass reading, take a slow walk around the outside and inside of the house/office. Carry a notebook and pen and scrutinize the environment. Use one of your extra floorplan copies to diagram the landscape, street and any other objects surrounding the house.

As you walk around the house take the following factors into account:

* **Smell**   Notice if the air is stagnant. Check
             for any unusual odors.
* **Sight**   Are there any features that turn you
             off? These can include overgrown
             vegetation, refuse and overall
             condition. Check the level of
             sunlight. Check the shape of the lot.

* **Sound**   Check for street noise. Ask about any
             disturbances from the neighbors.

* **Feeling**   This is a subjective feeling. Often
             times we get an intuitive feeling
             about places and people that we
             cannot explain.

* **Object**   This would include things you can touch
                  or feel such as noisy floorboards, loose
                  banisters and other potentially dangerous
                  features.

It is also useful to note that negative effects of Sha can take anywhere from 6 months to 1 year. Generally, the more serious the Sha the faster it will take effect.

Covered below are the most common external Sha factors that can occur in your neighborhood. There are other Sha factors, but these represent 95% of external Sha occurrences. Keep in mind that it's always easier to avoid problems from the beginning. Spend a little more time searching for the right house that doesn't have many negatives. We have offered you remedies for major problems. Still, many of them are only stop-gaps. They are designed only to minimize Sha, not eliminate it.

Finding a house with every aspect in harmony is almost impossible. Perfection is a commendable goal but impossible to find. You'll only make yourself crazy looking for the perfect home. It's kind of like the search for the Holy Grail. Many Feng Shui masters will advise that finding a home with up to a 75% all-around positive rating is an excellent house.

This house is located directly across from an oil storage facility. The visual, smell and noise factors would be most affected. The house has an obvious environmental Sha and should be avoided.

Adjacent Construction and Blocked Front Door

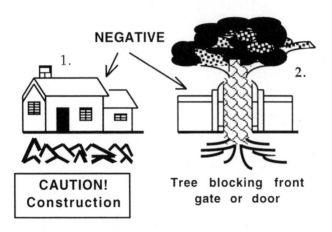

CAUTION!
Construction

Tree blocking front
gate or door

Problem 1:
Construction or excavation in front of a house. This type of problem may cause headaches and other physical pains.

Remedy:
Move out until construction is completed or place metal at the front-inside part of the house. This remedy will cancel the negative energy.

Problem 2:
Large tree, bush, pole or other permanent large object blocking the front door. Positive Chi flow is directed away from the front door causing poor health and business.

Remedy:
Remove the object. Construct a clear path from the front door to the street.

High-Tension Wires   Cemeteries

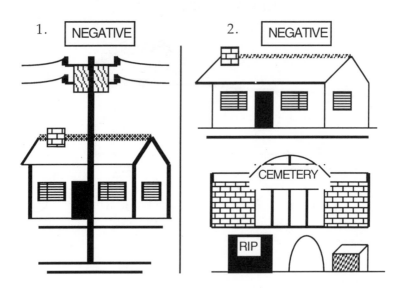

Problem 1:
The house is closer than 50 feet to high-tension wires. This Sha can cause a wide variety of serious health problems. The power of the electro-magnetic is so strong that it can't be completely eliminated.
Remedy:
Avoid these types of houses. If you can't move, place earth between the house and wires to reduce the negative energy.

Warning: This remedy is only a short-term measure and will not completely eliminate the Sha. Move as soon as possible.

Problem 2:
Your home or office is adjacent to a cemetery.
Remedy:
Strongly recommend that you avoid these homes. If you live in this kind of house, plan on moving as soon as possible.

Low-Rise Building Between High-Rises

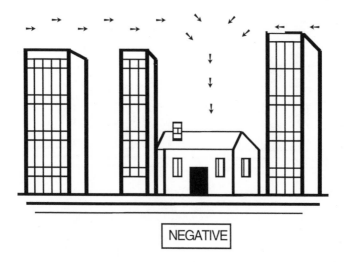

NEGATIVE

Problem:

This is a common environmental problem in areas with poor zoning regulations. A sense of pressure, discomfort and nervousness are common in these types of cases. The pressure is projected onto the house from the surrounding high-rises. There can be illness and bad luck associated with these residences.

Remedy:

Avoid moving into neighborhoods with single family homes next to large/tall commercial/residential buildings. You can plant trees around the house to reduce the pressure. This remedy will absorb much of the negative Chi. Find a house in an area that is planned for single family homes.

High-Rise Between Low-Rise Buildings

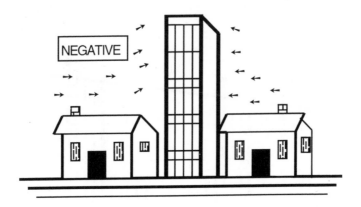

Problem:
Non-conforming buildings are considered bad Feng Shui. The same problem also affects a single home at the top of a hill. Illnesses and poor business fortunes are common in this environment. Often there is a feeling of discomfort and pressure. A high-rise will dominate the surrounding smaller buildings. Although this example is considered bad Feng Shui, it's better to dominate in a high-rise, than be dominated in a smaller, adjacent building.

Solution:
Avoid moving into a high-rise surrounded by low-rise buildings. Choose a high-rise surrounded by other high-rise buildings. Also avoid a home by itself at the top of a hill. If you can, plan trees around the high-rise. This will help reduce the pressure. Plant trees completely around a home if it's by itself at the top of a hill.

Large-Scale Additions

Use of Skylights

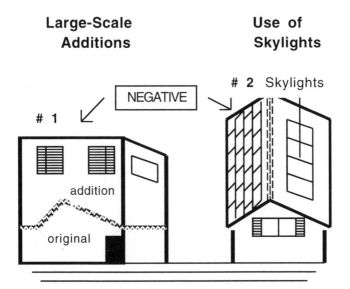

Problem #1:
Large scale additions that exceed the original house are bad Feng Shui. A new energy is created when the old roof is removed. The old foundation may not support the addition.

Solution:
Avoid homes with additions larger than the original house. Don't construct large additions onto an existing home.

Problem #2:
Excessive use of skylights may cause a Yang energy imbalance. There is excessive heat build-up. The strong sunlight also may cause headaches and hypertension.

Solution:
Don't build skylights that are larger than 1/5 the total area of the roof. Cover or remove unneeded skylights.

Positioning of Your Bed

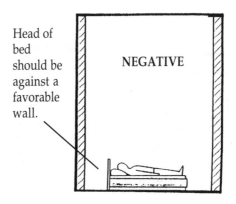

Head of bed should be against a favorable wall.

NEGATIVE

Problem:
Setting your bed in the center of the room may cause nervousness, anxiety, poor sleep and worry.

Solution:
Place the head of your bed against the wall. Choose the wall that is most favorable to you using the guidelines in chapter 8. Try to choose a wall that offers you peace and harmony.

Bedroom Mirror in Direct Line of Sight

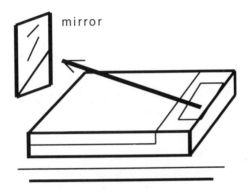

mirror

Problem:
The head of the bed is in a direct line of sight with a mirror. Poorly placed and excessive use of mirrors is considered bad Feng Shui. Mirrors reflect energy and can raise anxiety levels. Also avoid large, mirrored closet doors.

Solution:
Move the bed or mirror out of a direct line of sight from your pillow. Avoid placing mirrors onto your walls and closet doors.

Overhead Beams

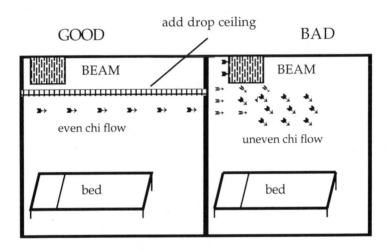

Problem:
A large ceiling beam over the bed (especially the pillow) may cause nervousness, poor sleep and anxiety. Ceiling beams disrupt Chi flow. Negative Chi can be projected onto the bed.

Remedy:
Install a drop ceiling that covers the overhead beam. If this isn't possible, move to another bedroom. If none of the previous remedies are possible, move your bed as far away from the beam as you can. As a rule, try to avoid homes that have large ceiling beams.

Direct Line From the Front Door
To the Bedroom

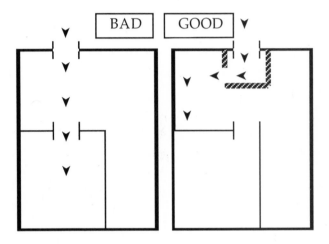

Problem:
A direct line from the front door to the bedroom is bad
Feng Shui. Negative energy is allowed to enter the
bedroom directly from the outside.

Remedy:
Redirect the negative energy away from the bedroom.
Construct a wall or use a wall unit, folding door, large
planter or any other tasteful piece of decor to affect the
change.

More Bed Positioning Analysis

Figure 1   Figure 2

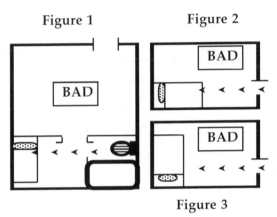

Figure 3

Problem   Figure 1:
Your pillow should not be in a direct line of sight with the commode. The toilet is considered to be negative.

Remedy:
Position bed away from a direct view of the commode.

Problem   Figures 2 and 3:
The head and vital organs of the body should not be in a direct line with the bedroom door. Negative energy entering the room may affect the occupant. Figures 2 and 3 are considered bad Feng Shui.

Remedy:
Position bed away from a direct line from the head and vital organs to the bedroom door.

Location of Fireplace and Kitchen

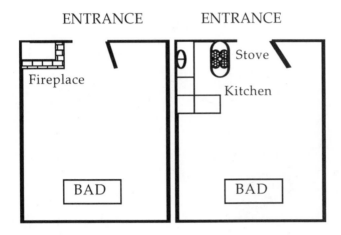

Problem:
Fireplace and kitchen next to the front door is unfavorable. Heat burns off positive Chi entering from the doorway. This condition can cause illness and poor business fortunes.

Remedy:
Install a floor to ceiling wall that physically separates the kitchen and fireplace (if used) away from the front door. Use another entrance if you can. Otherwise, avoid moving into homes with fireplaces and kitchens next to the entrance.

Eave, Wall Corner or Sharp Object
Pointed at Your House

Problem:
Eaves are the corner protrusions of roofs. Sharp corners of adjacent buildings are also bad Feng Shui. An adjacent eave or sharp corner, within 50 feet, should not be pointed at your house. Chi is projected onto the house in a negative manner. Bodily aches and pains are common with this problem.

Remedy:
Place a fish tank or large vase of water at the point where the eave hits the house (especially next to a window). Block the view of the eave with blinds or curtains. Avoid moving into homes that lay in the path of an eave (closer than 50 feet).

Incorrect   East-West
Bed   Positioning

Example: CHEN/SUN PERSONAL TRIGRAM

INCORRECT   CORRECT

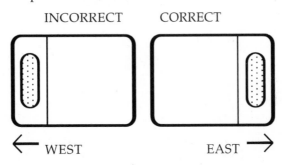

← WEST   EAST →

Problem:
The head of the bed for a Chen person is pointed in the "H" position. Using an incorrect bed position exposes a person to negative energy. Problems could include poor finances/career and possible robbery.

Remedy:
Position the head of your bed in a favorable direction. Use the East-West Chart in chapter 5 to find your best direction. Use one of the "A"-"D" positions if possible.

Lot   Shapes

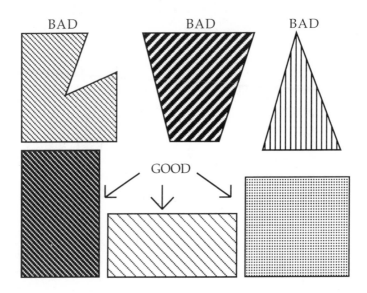

Problem:
Irregularly shaped houses and lots are considered bad
Feng Shui. Chi flow is negatively formed, especially in
triangle lots. Other irregular lots reduce positive energy
because of missing segments. Health and business
problems are common for those with homes on these
types of lots.

Remedy:
Stay with square or rectangular shaped lots when you
look for a new home. This is the best remedy.
Triangular shaped lots can be helped with the addition
of a pool or water fountain on the property. Water
helps absorb the negative energy shaped by the lot.

House/Street   Siting

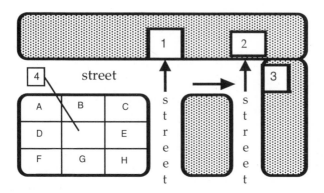

Problem:

#1. Avoid homes located at the end of the street. These also include cul de sac streets. These locations are frequently the sight of auto accidents. They are considered bad Feng Shui.

#2, #3. Don't buy a home that sits on a curve. Auto accidents often occur on curved streets. Check the traffic speed and flow. Ask about auto accidents in your neighborhood.

#4. Use East-West theory to analyze a block of houses. For example, analyze the entire housing tract if the homes were built at the same time. If you are selecting retail or commercial property, analyze the entire complex using East-West theory. Draw a grid over the entire development, just as you would for a single floorplan. Choose a lot based on your personal trigram. That way, your personal and house trigrams are the same. Having the same trigrams strengthens your positive Chi power.

SOME TIPS FOR HOMEBUYERS

High Ceilings. Try to avoid homes with excessively high ceilings. Cathedral ceilings increase negative energy and reduce positive energy in the room. Many contemporary homes have this feature. They are considered bad Feng Shui. The higher a ceiling is built, the more negative the energy is created. High Ceilings can give the occupants a feeling of loneliness and coldness.

Circular Bedrooms. Avoid bedrooms with a circular design. Chi energy is increased, resulting in hyperactivity, insomnia and nervousness. The energy created from a round bed or bedroom is good for sexual activities, and bad for rest and relaxation. An office may be circular, as energy and motion would be stimulated. A square or rectangular shape encourages peacefulness.

Hillside Homes. Avoid homes built into steep hillsides. There are obvious environmental problems as well as negative energy associated with this kind of location.

Water Runoff. Avoid homes with excessive water runoff. The runoff is usually dirty water. Dirty water passing in front of your house is very bad Feng Shui. Generally, these are homes built on a slope. The runoff can be on the street or through the property. This is an especially bad aspect for your finances. Find a home built on a flat lot.

Fixtures. Large chandeliers and other intrusive fixtures are bad Feng Shui. They are uncomfortable to sit under and can disrupt Chi flow.

Appliances. Minimize the number of electrical appliances in your home. Microwave ovens, stereos, large-screen televisions can be a health hazard in heavily used rooms. Definitely keep the electronics out of your bedroom. Consumer safety standards should be maintained at all times.

Try to minimize electrical appliances, especially in the bedroom. They give off excessive electro-magnetic radiation.

Shrubs. Remove dying plants or trees from your yard. They consume positive Chi and create negative energy.

Wind Chimes. Never hang a metal wind chime inside your home or in your patio, yard, windows or doors. Wind Chimes attract negative energy, and we strongly recommend against their use.

Wind Chimes in the Home.
Feng Shui advises removing from your home. They attract negative energy and traditionally signify illness.

PRACTICE EXERCISES

The following exercises are designed to reinforce the material presented in this chapter. Check your answers located in the back of the book. We recommend that you master any difficult ideas before progressing to the next chapter.

1. A man with a Li birthday has his pillow positioned toward the east. Is this good for peaceful sleep? Would there be a better position for sleep and rest?

2. A couple have a large screen television, stereo and computer set up in their bedroom. What do you think is the effect? What remedy would you recommend?

3. A family has a very dark hallway. People bump into things at night, and it's hard to find your way. What would you recommend?

4. A home has the front door, and the back door in a straight line. What would you recommend?

5. The kitchen of a home is next to the front door. Is this a Sha? Would you recommend any changes?

Answers can be found in the back of the book.

These high-tension pylons are about 60 feet from this house. Only recently have western scientists conceded that there may be a link between heavy exposure to electro-magnetic radiation and disease.

SUMMARY

1. Avoid trouble at the outset. When you look for a new home, don't move into a home with serious existing problems.

2. At this point you can use your knowledge of East-West theory and environmental Sha to analyze your living conditions.

3. Serious problems sometimes cannot be fixed adequately or not at all. Again, remember point #1.

4. Your environmental review begins with a slow walk around the house. Note any anomalies that are major or minor.

5. Position the head of your bed in the "D" position of your personal trigram. The "D" position promotes healthful sleep. You can use A, B, or C positions, if D is not possible.

6. Sha manifestations can be specific or vague. If something in your environment causes you anxiety or discomfort you probably can call it a Sha.

7. All negative Sha can be reduced to some degree by a master. If you are confused or unsure about a remedy, **always** consult a master.

Remove dead or dying trees especially from the front of your house. They are considered bad Feng Shui. Dying plants attract negative energy and consume positive energy.

Chapter Eight

PREDICT YOUR
PROSPEROUS FUTURE

Metal
One of the traditional Five Elements

This book has shown you several analytical methods used in classical Feng Shui theory. Let's review what we've covered so far:

* We have considered the importance of a homeowners

birthday. This is the **people** aspect of Feng Shui analysis.

* We have discussed the **environmental** factors in and around your home.

* We have also looked at the significance of the building itself. This is the **structure** component. You now know that the sitting direction of a house determines it's trigram name.

In this chapter we will examine the importance of time. This is the last component of basic Feng Shui analysis. We have used time in calculating your personal trigram. Now, we will now use time in a much more powerful way. Time will be used to more profoundly analyze the Feng Shui of a structure for a specific year.

Components of Feng Shui Analysis

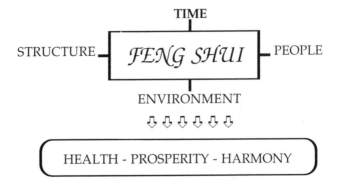

You may recall from an earlier chapter that each trigram represents many factors. A trigram can signify a number, element, part of the body, color and direction.

Our analysis has also used East-West theory after finding the direction and birthday of your house. Your birthday trigram was also analyzed.

In East-West theory, the trigram of the house takes precedence over the owner's trigram. Ideally, the trigram of the owner and the house should match. Using the method in this chapter, we progress to a more accurate and predictive analysis.

IMPORTANCE OF TIMING

The basis of analyzing yearly trends is based on the trigrams. We take from the trigrams a nine-part cycle from 1 to 9. A fundamental precept of Chinese philosophy is that life occurs within a cycle. A simple example are the four seasons of a year.

Once a house is completed, it retains the specific Chi force based on the sitting/facing direction. We learned in East-West analysis to grid a floorplan with a trigram. We will take the grid process one step further and analyze the contents of each particular grid for the current year. You also can use this analysis to review your past.

The annual analysis is accurate in corresponding with major events of your past. Of course, many people find the future analysis to be fascinating. You can use the method in this chapter for this as well. The East-West analysis provides a complete analysis of your home. Using the annual analysis provides additional information for specific a quadrant.

For example, a bedroom may have an "A" rating based on our East-West analysis. The overall energy of the room affects you in many positive ways. Still, if an unfavorable energy exists in the "A" quadrant for this year, you may experience some negative events based on the annual energy although the quadrant overall, is good for you. Also, if a positive energy enters the "A" quadrant for that year, you will have extra positive events based on the annual energy.

This chapter will show you how to predict with amazing accuracy, events that may occur in your life. You may need to read this chapter several times. Although the material is not difficult to learn, it's recommended that you double-check your analysis to catch any mistakes. Follow the easy steps in this chapter for an accurate analysis.

ANNUAL YEAR ANALYSIS

1. Find your floorplan grid that you used in previous chapters. Double-check that your grid and compass directions are accurate.

Chen Sample Floorplan

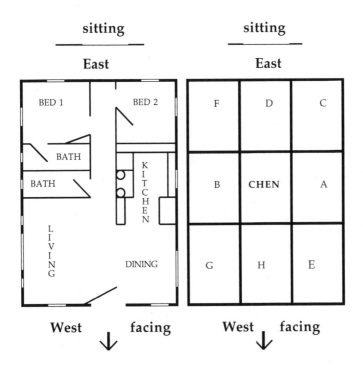

2. From the following chart, find the year that you want to analyze. Next to the year is the annual number. For this example, we'll use **1993**. Remember to use the Chinese Lunar calendar from February 5 to February 4 of each year. Each number has a different meaning.

Annual Number from 1900 to 2004

YEAR	NBR.	YEAR	NBR.	YEAR	NBR.
1900	1	1901	9	1902	8
1903	7	1904	6	1905	5
1906	4	1907	3	1908	2
1909	1	1910	9	1911	8
1912	7	1913	6	1914	5
1915	4	1916	3	1917	2
1918	1	1919	9	1920	8
1921	7	1922	6	1923	5
1924	4	1925	3	1926	2
1927	1	1928	9	1929	8
1930	7	1931	6	1932	5
1933	4	1934	3	1935	2
1936	1	1937	9	1938	8
1939	7	1940	6	1941	5
1942	4	1943	3	1944	2
1945	1	1946	9	1947	8
1948	7	1949	6	1950	5
1951	4	1952	3	1953	2
1954	1	1955	9	1956	8
1957	7	1958	6	1959	5
1960	4	1961	3	1962	2
1963	1	1964	9	1965	8
1966	7	1967	6	1968	5
1969	4	1970	3	1971	2
1972	1	1973	9	1974	8
1975	7	1976	6	1977	5
1978	4	1979	3	1980	2
1981	1	1982	9	1983	8
1984	7	1985	6	1986	5
1987	4	1988	3	1989	2
1990	1	1991	9	1992	8
1993	*7*	1994	6	1995	5
1996	4	1997	3	1998	2
1999	1	2000	9	2001	8
2002	7	2003	6	2004	5

3. Place the annual number in the center of your trigram. Place the next higher number in the trigram box as shown in the following grid. If you use number 9, start at number 1 in the next grid.

Chen Floorplan with East-West "A-H" Grid and Annual Numbers for 1993

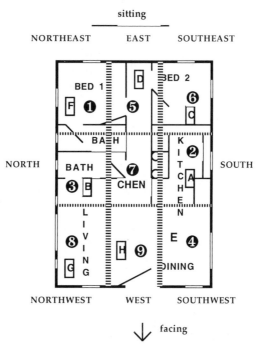

Remember, the annual number goes in the center of your floorplan grid. You start back at 1 after number 9. The laying in of the numbers goes in this sequence:

a.   Annual number in the center.
b.   Next number in the Northwest grid.
c.   Next number in the West grid.
d.   Next number in the Northeast grid.

e.   Next number in the South grid.
f.   Next number in the North grid.
g.   Next number in the Southwest grid.
h.   Next number in the East grid.
i.   Next number in the Southeast grid.

Using our example, if your annual number is 7:

Northwest 8	North 3	Northeast 1
West 9	Center 7	East 5
Southwest 4	South 2	Southeast 6

4. Use the number analysis chart to analyze each quadrant of your house. You can use the annual number combined with the A-H rating system covered in chapter 6.

Trigram   Mathematical   Interpretation

Number   **Interpretation**

1   Suggests a powerful position and material wealth.

2   This number can suggest various bodily
         pains, sickness and poor health.

3   You can be open to gossip, rumors,
         arguments and lawsuits.

4   There is the possibility of strong career
         advancement and promotions, scholastic
         achievement, communication talent and
         high creative aptitude.

5   Generally, you are prone to accidents and
         assorted bodily pains.

6   Strong potential for wealth and a high-
         level position, possibly without any
         authority.

7   You can be the victim of slander, gossip
         and arguments with this number. You are
         also susceptible to robbery and bleeding.

8   A good indicator of fame and a good
         reputation. You also can find yourself
         with a fortune.

9   This number intensifies the East-West
         rating with which it's paired.

Notice that 1, 4, 6, and 8 are positive in nature. Numbers 2, 3, 5 and 7 are negatively aspected. Number 9 is neutral by itself, but can be positive or negative depending on the East-West rating (A-H).

Now, let's look at our sample house and analyze each quadrant of the floorplan. Many rooms will have 2 quadrants. Keep this in mind as you analyze each room. The entrance and master bedroom are the most important quadrants. You should start your analysis with these two quadrants.

BEDROOM ANALYSIS:

Bedroom 2 has a "C" East-West rating and a "6" annual number. Bedroom 2 has a positive rating in terms of East-West and annual number analysis. The East-West analysis rates it a good room for family harmony and public image. Annual analysis rates the bedroom as good for wealth this year.

Bedroom 1 has a good annual number (1), but a poor East-West rating (F). A suggestion would be to use bedroom 1 as a home office for this year. Number 1 shows wealth and position and this would be one way you could take advantage of the annual trend.

RECOMMENDATION: Use bedroom 1 as the master bedroom.

ENTRANCE ANALYSIS:

The entrance has an unfavorable East-West rating (H), and a neutral annual rating (9). The "H" East-West rating indicates poor career and financial possibilities as well as potential robberies. The annual "9" would tend to reinforce the negative East-West rating.

RECOMMENDATION: Use the main entrance as little as possible for this year. Try to use a side or rear entrance if you have one.

KITCHEN ANALYSIS:

The kitchen has an "A" East-West rating and a "2" annual rating. The "A" is favorable, but the "2" is negative. The south quadrant also contains part of the stove.

RECOMMENDATION: The stove (and microwave if present) will burn off the energies in this quadrant. You will lose your positive energy and negative annual energy. Therefore, the kitchen is evaluated as a neutral part of this house.

OTHER ROOM ANALYSIS:
Examine the space between bedroom 1 and bedroom 2. This is the East quadrant that has a favorable East-West rating (D), but an unfavorable annual number (5). Number 5 usually reflects itself through personal accidents, injuries and pain. This number is the most powerful of the negative numbers and should always be remedied if possible.

RECOMMENDATION: Use the reductive cycle to lessen the negative influences of number 5. In chapter 5 we learned that "5" is associated with the element earth. To lessen the effects of negative "5", we use the reductive cycle. Place a metal object in the number 5 quadrant (east) to remedy the negative energy. You also may place an aquarium in the east quadrant. During this twenty year cycle (1984-2003), water will enhance the wood energy present in the east quadrant (productive cycle).

PRACTICE EXERCISES

Use the Chen floorplan in this chapter for the following practice exercises.

a.   Which quadrant does annual number "5" go to in 1994?

b.   Which is the better bedroom, a quadrant with F-4 or one with D-5?

c.   Where would you put metal in 1996?

d.   If annual number 3 came into my master bedroom, how could I reduce the negative energy?

Answers can be found at the end of the book.

Houses next to churches should be avoided.

SUMMARY

1. Use your floorplan that you used in chapter 6.

2. Find the year you want to analyze from the annual number chart.

3. Lay in the numbers based on the order shown in this chapter.

4. Remember to start at 1 after you reach 9.

5. Use the annual number analysis chart and the East-West rating chart to evaluate each room.

6. Decide if a remedy is needed and check with the elemental cycles (reductive, domination, productive) for the correct element remedy.

7. Always double-check your work for mistakes.

8. Use the Chinese Lunar calendar to find your annual number (February 5 to February 4).

These vases from a furniture store will make a
powerful earth remedy. The larger the object, the
more strength it will have as a remedy.

Chapter Nine

MAKING FENG SHUI WORK FOR YOU

Wood
One of the Traditional Five elements

Congratulations!   I hope, you've made it this far without a brain overload. We've covered much ground. Maybe your impression is one of confusion. Take heart, with some practice and review you can master the art of Feng Shui.

This concluding chapter will put all the parts together. A step-by-step work flow is provided to help you. Use the following flow chart on your first few house readings. This will help free your mind from procedure. You will be better able to concentrate on the analysis.

Work Flow

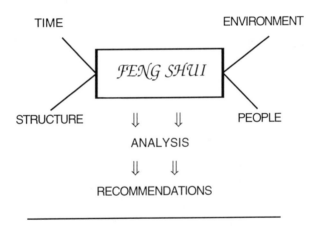

STEP BY STEP ANALYSIS

Step 1 **TIME**

a. Find the date the subject house was completed.

House construction completed: _____

Step 2 **ENVIRONMENT**

a. Do a walk-around of the subject house. Interior and exterior environmental factors should be noted. Use the methods explained in chapter 7.

Interior Environment:

ceilings stairs	flooring	electrical
history	cleanliness	fixtures
decor	furniture	moisture
lighting	ventilation	temperature
floorplan	kitchen	bedrooms
bathrooms	noise	smell
appliances		

Exterior Environment:

High-tension wires	fencing	landscaping
sewage	run-off	pad
configuration	traffic	noise
neighbors	cleanliness	smell
adjacent structures		

Step 3 PEOPLE

Find the birthdays of the owners of the subject house. Use the birth chart in chapter 5 to find their personal trigram.

Husband's birthday: _____

Husband's trigram: _____

Wife's birthday: _____

Wife's trigram: _____

Step 4 STRUCTURE

a. Find the date the house was completed (step 1).

b. Find the facing and sitting directions of the house.

c. Draw a floorplan of the subject house.

d. Use the East-West method from chapter 6 to rate each quadrant of your floorplan (A-H) based on the direction of the house.

e. Add in the annual numbers to your floorplan grid (chapter 8).

Step 5 PRELIMINARY ANALYSIS

a. Use the East-West Method to grid the subject house using the **owner's** birthday (trigram).

b. Use the East-West Method to grid the subject house using the **house's** birthday (trigram).

c. The trigram of the house takes precedence over the trigram of the owner's.

d. Using the East-West Method in Chapters 5 and 6, grid the rooms from A-H.

e. Find your best and worst rooms using the East-West Method. Change rooms where needed.

Step 6 ANNUAL ANALYSIS

Use chapter 4 to help you analyze the quadrants of the subject house. Knowledge of the elemental cycles is necessary for a remedy. The number analysis chart in chapter 8 should be used for analysis. The annual number will take precedence over the East-West house and personal energy.

Step 7 **FINAL ANALYSIS/REMEDIES**

Remedies using the elemental cycles should be prescribed (chapter 4). Consider the environmental factors that need to be corrected. Finally, go through and check your analysis at least one more time. An incorrect Feng Shui analysis may be worse than no analysis.

The house on the far left sits lower than the house across the street. The energy of the lower house is reversed, which may create negative energy.

SUMMARY

If you are serious about mastering Feng Shui, read as many houses as you can. Attend seminars given by the American Feng Shui Institute (address in the back of the book). Join the American Feng Shui Society and network with like-thinking individuals.

Read the advanced Feng Shui books by the same author to enrich your breadth and depth of knowledge. Subscribe to the Green Dragon Newsletter and learn from interesting case studies. Your journey has only begun!

Appendix A - Quiz Answers

Chapter 3

Fill in the blanks on the following chart:

Trigram	Direction	Number	Element
Chien	Northwest	6	Metal
K'un	Southwest	2	Earth
Chen	East	3	Wood
Sun	Southeast	4	Wood
K'an	North	1	Water
Li	South	9	Fire
Ken	Northeast	8	Earth
Tui	West	7	Metal

Chapter 6

Practice Exercise:

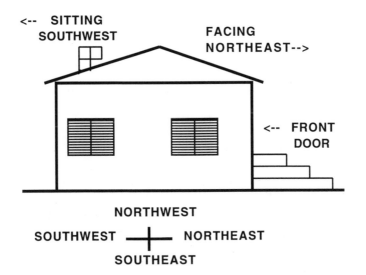

Chapter 6 Continued

1. What is the facing direction? **Northeast**
2. What is the sitting direction? **Southwest**

Practice Exercises:

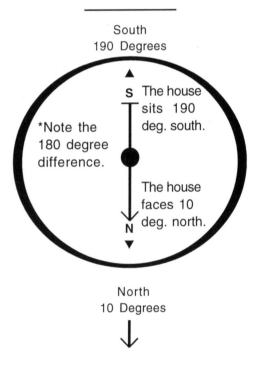

South
190 Degrees

S The house
   sits 190
   deg. south.

*Note the
180 degree
difference.

The house
faces 10
deg. north.

N

North
10 Degrees

1. Refer to the compass pictured above. This is the
   facing direction (north) of a house. What is the
   trigram? **Li**

2. A house sits at 60 degrees (Use your compass).
   What is the trigram? **Chen (sits to the east)**

Chapter 6 Continued

Practice Exercises:

Example #1 Lay in the letters A - H for this house. Use the Li chart from the East Group trigram chart.

LI PRACTICE FLOORPLAN

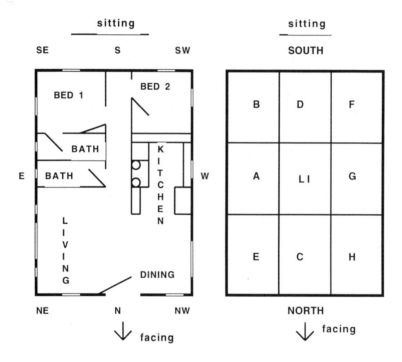

Chapter 6 Continued

Example #2   Lay in the letters A - H for the
following Tui office. Use the Tui chart from the West
Group trigram chart.

TUI PRACTICE OFFICE FLOORPLAN

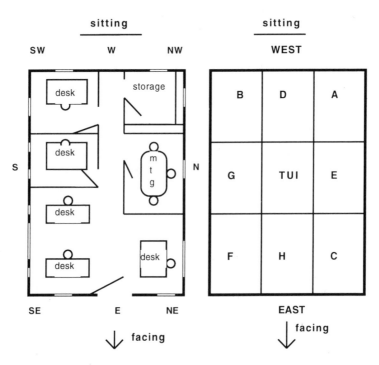

Chapter 7

Practice Exercises:

1. A man with a Li birthday has his pillow positioned toward the east. Is this good for peaceful sleep? Would there be a better position for sleep and rest? Better for business. Move pillow to the south.

2. A couple have a large screen television, stereo and computer set up in their bedroom. What do you think is the effect? What would you recommend as remedy? Large electro-magnetic radiation field. Remove all the electronics from the bedroom.

3. A family has a very dark hallway. People bump into things at night, and it's hard to find your way. What would you recommend? Add skylights or additional lighting.

4. A home has the front door, and the back door in a straight line. What would you recommend? Add a wall or room divider/bookcase to block the view to the bedroom.

5. The kitchen of a home is next to the front door. Is this a Sha? Would you recommend any changes? Yes, a stove near the entrance can burn off good energy. Construct a wall between the door and stove/kitchen.

Chapter 8

Chen Floorplan with East-West "A-H" Grid and Annual Numbers for 1993

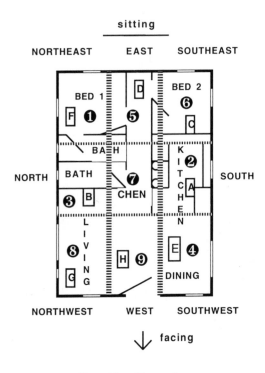

Practice Exercises:

Use the Chen floorplan above for the practice exercises.

a. What quadrant does annual number "5" go in 1994?
    Southeast

b. Which is the better bedroom, a quadrant with F-4
    or D-5? F-4, the annual number takes
    precedence, especially if it's a negative number.

Chapter 8 Continued

c. Where would I put metal in 1996? Northwest

d. If annual number 3 came into my master bedroom, how could I reduce the negative energy? Metal

The house in the center of the photo is on pylons perched over the side of a hill. This house would be bad Feng Shui. Choose a house that has a flat lot with good water drainage.

This house has an excellent front design. From the front door there is a clear path to the street. The house is on a slight rise and avoids being dominated by an adjacent house.

APPENDIX B

Personal Trigram Chart

1950 - 1999

YEAR	MALE	FEMALE	YEAR	MALE	FEMALE
1950	Kun	Kan	1975	Tui	Ken
1951	Sun	Kun	1976	Chien	Li
1952	Chen	Chen	1977	Kun	Kan
1953	Kun	Sun	1978	Sun	Kun
1954	Kan	Ken	1979	Chen	Chen
1955	Li	Chien	1980	Kun	Sun
1956	Ken	Tui	1981	Kan	Ken
1957	Tui	Ken	1982	Li	Chien
1958	Chien	Li	1983	Ken	Tui
1959	Kun	Kan	1984	Tui	Ken
1960	Sun	Kun	1985	Chien	Li
1961	Chen	Chen	1986	Kun	Kan
1962	Kun	Sun	1987	Sun	Kun
1963	Kan	Ken	1988	Chen	Chen
1964	Li	Chien	1989	Kun	Sun
1965	Ken	Tui	1990	Kan	Ken
1966	Tui	Ken	1991	Li	Chien
1967	Chien	Li	1992	Ken	Tui
1968	Kun	Kan	1993	Tui	Ken
1969	Sun	Kun	1994	Chien	Li
1970	Chen	Chen	1995	Kun	Kan
1971	Kun	Sun	1996	Sun	Kun
1972	Kan	Ken	1997	Chen	Chen
1973	Li	Chien	1998	Kun	Sun
1974	Ken	Tui	1999	Kan	Ken

This ornamental Chinese fighting sword makes an
excellent metal remedy and wall decoration.

Water

When the shoe fits, the foot is forgotten.
When the belt fits, the belly is forgotten.
When the heart is right, "for" and "against" are forgotten.

Chuang Tzu

ORDER FORM

Write or call for the following:

Feng Shui: Discover Money, Health and Love..$13.95

Send me The Green Dragon Feng Shui Newsletter and add me to your mailing list for upcoming seminars, books and products.. Free!!

Genuine Chinese Compass translated to English including full instructions and deluxe carrying case... $89.95

Send me information for a personal consultation ....price varies

☎ **Telephone orders: Call: 310/285-8616**

Name: _____

Address: _____

City, State, Zip: _____

Please send me the following: _____ $ _____

Please send me the following: _____ $ _____
Shipping: Book Rate $2.00 for the first book and .75
for each additional book. Air Mail $3.50 per book : $ _____

Calif. Residents add 6.75% tax: $ _____

Amount Enclosed: $ _____

Please enclose personal check, money order or cashiers check

Send to: Dragon Publishing
1223 Broadway #231
Santa Monica, Ca. 90404

Master Larry Sang applying his signature
"chop" to some recently finished calligraphy.

ORDER FORM

Write or call for the following:

Feng Shui: Discover Money, Health and Love..$13.95

Send The Green Dragon Feng Shui Newsletter and add me to your mailing list for upcoming seminars, books and products... Free!!

Genuine Chinese Compass translated to English including full instructions and deluxe carrying case.. $89.95

Send me information for a personal consultation ....price varies

☎ **Telephone orders: Call: 310/285-8616**

Name: _____

Address: _____

City, State, Zip: _____

Please send me the following: _____ $ _____

Please send me the following: _____ $ _____

Shipping: Book Rate $2.00 for the first book and .75 for each additional book. Air Mail $3.50 per book : $ _____

Calif. Residents add 6.75% tax: $ _____

Amount Enclosed: $ _____

Please enclose personal check, money order or cashiers check

Send to: Dragon Publishing
                     1223 Broadway #231
                     Santa Monica, Ca. 90404